The Complete Guide to Owning a Deaf Dog

Amanda Brahlek

Publication Data

Amanda Brahlek

The Complete Guide to Owning a Deaf Dog – First edition.

Summary: "Successfully raising a deaf dog from puppy to old age" – Provided by publisher.

ISBN: 978-1-954288-11-9

[1. Deaf Dogs – Non-Fiction] I. Title.

This book has been written with the published intent to provide accurate and author-itative information in regard to the subject matter included. While every reasonable precaution has been taken in preparation of this book the author and publisher expressly disclaim responsibility for any errors, omissions, or adverse effects arising from the use or application of the information contained inside. The techniques and suggestions are to be used at the reader's discretion and are not to be considered a substitute for professional veterinary care. If you suspect a medical problem with your dog, consult your veterinarian.
Design by Sorin Rădulescu
First hardcover edition, 2021

TABLE OF CONTENTS

INTRODUCTION

You may be picking up this book because you're interested in adopting a deaf dog, or you may have already brought your deafie home. This book is also helpful if your beloved dog's hearing is beginning to fail, and you're looking for advice. No matter the reason—take a deep breath—you've got this! This book will provide you with a better understanding of what it takes to care for a deaf dog.

Owning a deaf dog has been more rewarding than I ever imagined, but at times, it hasn't been easy. In this book, I aim to give you the full picture: the good and the bad. More importantly, I hope to narrow the learning curve by giving you practical advice to make caring for a deaf dog easier.

When I adopted my spunky deaf dog, Natchez, the adoption coordinator told me that he would make an excellent running partner. He also said deaf dogs didn't take much more work than hearing dogs. I soon learned that both of these things weren't 100% accurate. Before deciding to commit to Natchez, I scoured the internet watching YouTube training videos and reading any information I could find. After days of research, I just couldn't find

Natch & Amanda

the answers I needed and couldn't grasp exactly what it would be like to care for a deaf dog. Over the years, I realized that caring for and training Natchez would have been much easier if I knew what to expect. That's where this book comes in.

Natch getting trained

I clearly remember when I got home with Natchez; he was a maniac. He immediately climbed onto side tables, broke lamps, and when leashed, pulled like an ox on steroids. I honestly considered returning him to the shelter. I even contacted the adoption coordinator. My family encouraged me to be patient and keep him. Within a couple of days, we had a breakthrough when Natchez learned to sit. Now, the thought of living without my beloved deaf dog breaks my heart.

To pay it forward, I have fostered deaf dogs to help them learn hand signs, learn to live in a home, become more adoptable, and find loving homes.

Looking back on my life with Natchez, I would make the same choice to adopt him if I had the choice to do over. And, yes, adopting a deaf dog is scary, which is why my choice may not be the right decision for everyone. Deaf dogs are more work, but they offer love and companionship that is nearly indescribable. Because of their disability, these quirky dogs form a unique bond with their owners. Deafies will make you laugh, smile, and fill your home with love. As I write, Natchez is sleeping soundly and snuggly pressed against my leg, and I wouldn't want it any other way.

If you're considering adding a deaf dog to your family, this book should guide you to a decision that is best for you. I hope if you do decide to adopt a deafie that my insight will help make raising and training your new pup a positive experience.

CHAPTER 1
Getting the Story Straight

A History of Deaf Canines

The story of deaf dogs isn't one that is well documented. Luckily, there are some famous deaf dogs that made enough of an impression to warrant their spot in history. Unfortunately, there are also many deafies who were not given the opportunity to make their splash in the history books.

Photo Courtesy of Tracey Gant

A Change in Attitude: Bob Parker and Buddy, the Deaf Dog

Bob Parker, a gentleman who reminds me a bit of Mr. Rogers, dropped out of high school when he was seventeen to join the army. He fought in both World Wars, and he also fought for a cause he believed in: the idea that deaf dogs had value. Mr. Parker used his deaf dog, Buddy, to educate and change the minds of those that believed deaf dogs were untrainable.

Bob Parker didn't set out to become an advocate for deaf dogs. In fact, he found Buddy strolling along the plains in Kansas. While most people would have continued on after Buddy snarled and tried to bite, Bob didn't let a little spunk and attitude deter him. He brought Buddy home, and the two eventually formed an incredible bond.

FUN FACT

Buddy the Dog

In the 1950s, a deaf dog named Buddy was trained by his owner, Bob Parker, to inspire students at the Kansas School for the Deaf. The duo created an act in Olathe, Kansas, to svvhowcase Buddy's talents and inspire deaf children by showing that Buddy could be great despite, and perhaps because of, his deafness. Photos of Buddy the Deaf Dog can be found in the Kansas School for the Deaf archives.

As their bond grew, Buddy and Bob's ability to communicate grew as well. In the 1950s, Mr. Parker decided it was time to show off how trainable Buddy was by presenting a one-dog-performance in which Buddy completed complex and entertaining routines on stage, including playing the piano. Maybe most impressive of all, Buddy often wore costumes while doing so. He was known for his hat.

Soon, Buddy began touring. He and Mr. Parker went to schools, including schools for deaf children. Together, this pair inspired deaf youth and also brought awareness to the abilities of deaf dogs.

The Dark Side of Deaf Dog History: Euthanasia

While documentation on what happened to many deaf puppies is difficult to find, there is a lot of evidence suggesting deaf dogs were not kept around very long. It's likely that euthanasia of deafies coincided with breeding practices that developed centuries ago and came into full swing in the latter part of the 19th century. Sadly, this practice continued within American breeding clubs until the 2000s and still is today in many parts of the world.

Many people mistakenly believe there has been an increase in the occurrence or births of deafies over the past three decades. This is likely not the case, though. We see more deaf dogs now because there is more awareness of their existence through social media and the internet. Furthermore, <u>more deaf dogs survive to adulthood</u> because fewer are destroyed soon after birth.

All of this to say, many breeders chose to euthanize deaf puppies as recently as 2016. Why? Deaf dogs were not very profitable and often seen as difficult to train. Additionally, breeders did not want a congenital disorder passed along, while others believed if buyers were to see a deaf dog among the litter, it would negatively affect the breeder's reputation. Views like these are made clear in breeding guidelines and policies on how to handle deaf dogs. One of the most prominent and poignant examples being that of the Dalmatian Club of America's position on deaf puppies.

Remember the movie *101 Dalmatians*? The demand for Dalmatian puppies skyrocketed after the movie came out, which lead to excessive breeding and a rise in the occurrence of deaf Dalmatians. Dalmatians have the highest rates of congenital deafness; about 30% of Dalmatians are born deaf. At the time, the Dalmatian Club of America required breeders who were registered with them to put down deaf puppies. Their policy stated, "deaf pups should always be humanely destroyed by a Veterinarian" and that if "a deaf pup is inadvertently placed, it should be replaced with a hearing pup."

They also suggested, "If you are the owner of a deaf dalmatian, and are having problems with the dog, don't feel 'guilty' about it. Consider starting over with a healthy, hearing pup. (And DO have the deaf dog put down)." They further said, "If you are a veterinarian, please advise your clients to put down any deaf pups they may have bred. PLEASE do not make it any more difficult for your client by suggesting that perhaps a 'special' home might be found. With the enormous surplus of unwanted dogs in this country, there is no need to preserve dogs with problems such as deafness." While these quotes have been practically wiped clean from the Dalmatian Club of America's website, their effect can still be felt.

Fortunately, these guidelines changed in 2016, and the Dalmatian Club of America is now one of the leading funders of research regarding the genetics related to deafness.

Their current position is that deaf Dalmatians should be fixed and cared for, although they do warn "Deaf pups should NEVER be bred from. Deaf Dalmatians can be harder to raise, difficult to control (they are often hit by cars when they 'escape') and often become snappish or overly aggressive, especially when startled."

Until 2013, the Australian Shepherd Club of America held the position that "white-factored puppies" should be culled and euthanized immediately after birth.

While this was often the fate of dogs born congenitally deaf, the same sad reality often occurred to dogs that went deaf later on in life.

Many dog owners believed that aging dogs naturally became more obstinate because their dogs were less likely to come when called or respond to their names and commands. We now recognize these as signs of age-related hearing loss. They justified putting these deaf dogs down because they were more difficult to manage. Funny enough, deafness may be one factor in the origin of the adage "old dogs can't learn new tricks" because old dogs have more difficulty hearing the commands.

Often, hunting dogs experienced shorter lives if their owners chose euthanasia rather than retirement (which was the case more often than not). Hunting dogs lost and still lose their hearing due to the repeated sound trauma of gun blasts. Sadly, many owners saw the inability to perform and respond to commands as justification for euthanasia. Unfortunately, articles still emerge regarding this practice, including how Galgos, a Spanish hunting breeding, are left to die after their hunting ability wanes.[1]

The misnomer that deaf dogs were aggressive and untrainable made deaf dogs unlikely candidates for adoption and often justified euthanasia for many breeders.

Sadly, this attitude continues today. Physical issues, old age, and aggression continue to be the leading reasons dogs are put to sleep.

Compared to a century ago, deaf dogs have come a long way in terms of how they're viewed. It's now more common for breeders to bring their deaf puppies to the pound or shelters after the other puppies have been re-homed, and with education, many breeders are beginning to practice more responsible breeding practices which can lessen the occurrence of deafness.

How Common is Deafness in Dogs?

Deafness in dogs may be congenital or acquired through hearing loss. As you can probably guess, hearing loss is very common as dogs age. Many senior dogs experience partial hearing loss, while others completely lose their hearing. Acquired deafness is the most common form of canine deafness.

As for dogs that are born deaf, the prevalence varies depending on the breed. When it comes to double-merle dogs, recent studies show 25% are born deaf (previous studies with smaller groups of double-merles showed the number to be as high as 54%). For single-merle dogs, 9% are born either bilaterally

---

1   Natasha Daly, "Traditional Hunting Dogs Are Left to Die En Masse in Spain." National Geographic, October 2016.

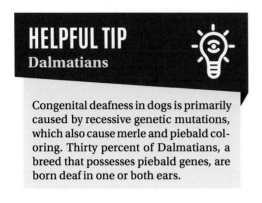

HELPFUL TIP
Dalmatians

Congenital deafness in dogs is primarily caused by recessive genetic mutations, which also cause merle and piebald coloring. Thirty percent of Dalmatians, a breed that possesses piebald genes, are born deaf in one or both ears.

or unilaterally deaf. As an example, Border Collies have about a 2.3% prevalence of deafness.[2]

This is all to say that with over 70 million dogs in the United States it's difficult to pinpoint how many deaf dogs there really are. Some estimates suggest there are about 35,000, although that number seems a bit low. The American Kennel Club estimates that 5-10% of dogs are either partially or fully deaf, which is significantly higher.

I personally see more and more deaf dogs on a regular basis. I've even been at the dog park with three or four other deafies tromping about, which in a town of 60,000 seems like a lot.

So, if you're considering adopting a deaf dog, and you're wondering if your dog will be the only deaf dog at the dog park, chances are he will be at times, but not always. If you're looking for a group of deaf dog owners for support, be reassured: you won't be short of options.

Clearing Up Misconceptions: Aggression, Inbreeding, and Obstinance

Misconceptions that deaf dogs are aggressive and untrainable still linger. Much of this has to do with misunderstanding deaf dogs, trauma, and lack of proper socialization.

I just read an article by George M. Strain, PhD and professor of Neuroscience in Louisiana State University's School of Veterinary Medicine, that said that for every success story of raising a deaf dog, there are two that result in incredible problems. Strain went on to explain that he would not want deaf dogs around his family because one cannot predict which deaf dogs will develop aggression. Upon a closer look at this study, the researcher only had firsthand experience with five deaf dogs, which were kept strictly for the purpose of breeding studies.[3] In my opinion, this does not seem to be a fair assessment.

---

2 George M. Strain et al., "Prevalence of Deafness in Dogs Heterozygous or Homozygous for the Merle Allele." Journal of Veterinary Internal Medicine 23, no. 2 (2009): 282-286.

3 George M. Strain, "Discussion on Dalmatian Deafness," LSU, accessed December 21, 2020, https://www.lsu.edu/deafness/strain1.html.

So why do deaf dogs get such a bad rap?

Deaf dogs often do not receive proper socialization, training, or care for their needs. Many others become the targets of frustration and abuse by pet owners who do not know their dog is deaf and so believe their dog is just stubborn and "won't listen." These dogs often wind up in shelters where they experience the trauma of being ownerless, homeless, confused, and stressed. This can result in anxiety once they're adopted out.

Deaf dogs tend to be jumpy and react with surprise when startled. This can, in-turn, startle a person. Sometimes, the nervousness of a deaf dog can make it appear erratic. But many people expect a deaf dog to react the way a hearing dog would, and that's simply not the case.

Aggression

Are there aggressive deaf dogs? Of course, just as there are aggressive hearing dogs. It's all about how the dog has been treated, since aggression is a learned behavior.

Deaf dogs have loud barks since they can't hear themselves. This often makes them very intimidating to strangers. My dog loves to bark while running and playing with other dogs. He also has a classic "deaf dog's bark," which is tonally rough and very, very loud. Sometimes other pup parents think this means he's aggressive when, in reality, he's just loud.

Some deafies may compensate for their anxiety by trying to appear tough or defensive. They will posture by slapping the ground and barking but quickly retreat when approached. My deaf dog often does this with strangers. Sometimes he barks at strangers but won't look directly at them because he's really just a scaredy-cat.

Finally, I should point out that deaf dogs sometimes play rough. While this isn't actually aggression, it can be a bit scary. Puppies (and kitties) learn about limits to how hard they should nip, bite, paw, and generally play from their littermates' vocal cues. Since deafies don't hear these cues, they don't necessarily learn the normal restraint when playing. Luckily, with a little training, deaf dogs can be taught to play nicely.

Trainability and Obstinance

When training a deaf dog, it's easy to see how some people think they're untrainable. Like with hearing dogs, though, it's all about effective communication—in the case of deafies, using hand signals and body language. All it takes is a willingness to think a little differently and learn a new way of communicating.

In my experience, Natchez learned commands much quicker than my hearing dog. Natchez learned to sit in a matter of minutes. Of course, this is likely because he's extremely food-motivated and eager to please, but speaking with other deaf dog owners, they often say their dogs learned quickly.

I also like to tell people about Ghost, a stray deaf dog who was scheduled to be euthanized. Ghost seemed hyper to most potential adopters until he was adopted by veteran military K-9 handler Barb Davenport. Barb saw the potential in Ghost and worked with him until he became qualified to train as a K-9 narcotics dog.

Deaf dogs are anything but obstinate. They often desperately want to please their owners. When Natchez learned to sit, it was like I lit a spark in him. He always looks to me or my husband for his next command, and he's learned commands that our hearing dog has yet to master.

Are Deaf Dogs the Product of Inbreeding?

This is a myth. While congenital deafness is the result of an inherited disorder and could be the result of inbreeding, it is often not caused by inbreeding. Instead, inherited deafness is passed by the mother and father dog both having the gene that results in deafness, not because the parents are closely related.

Common Appearance & Pigment Deficiency

Dogs that lose their hearing do not all look the same. Hearing loss can happen to all canines: big and small, chubby or tall. That said, congenital deafness is often linked to specific genetic markers—specifically, the two pigmentation genes that result in a dog's coat pattern and coloration. Because of this, a very high percentage of deaf dogs have pigment deficiency. This means they often have white coats and blue eyes.

Deafies' skin can also appear pinker. Sometimes they look like they have pink circles surrounding their eyes. This is often because their eyelashes are white or transparent.

Deaf dogs can also have dappled or patchy coloration on their noses. The result is pigmentation in some spots but not others, creating a patchwork of pink and black or brown. My dog's nose has been described as looking like a cow's hide, the technical term for these adorable noses is "butterfly" noses.

Some deaf dogs retain the pigment in their eyes or one eye.

All of this is to say that you cannot identify a deaf dog simply based on appearance, but you will notice a pattern that most deafies have, namely pale, white, or mostly white coats and blue eyes. Of course, there are deaf dogs with full coloration.

Photo Courtesy
of Janet Santilli

Signs, Symptoms, and Diagnosis

I get asked all the time, "How did you know your dog is deaf?" or "Are you sure he's deaf?" I always respond by saying that I knew he was deaf before I adopted him and that the veterinarian at the shelter diagnosed him. The process of discovering your dog or puppy is deaf may come as more of a surprise, though, since I often hear of people that adopt a new puppy only to discover their dog is deaf months later.

Is your dog deaf or just ignoring you? In this section, you will learn the signs that your dog is congenitally deaf, partially deaf, or losing his hearing.

Signs Your Dog is Going Deaf

If your dog has stopped listening to you or has become more stubborn, there's a good chance that he just can't hear you. As dogs age, the nerves in their ears tend to weaken and deteriorate over time. If your dog shows any of the following symptoms, it's a good idea to take him to the vet and have his hearing tested:

- Decreased response to auditory cues like opening and closing the front door, jingling the leash, or calling your dog's name.
- Sleeping more deeply and not waking to noise.
- More anxiety when you leave and confusion like being surprised you are home. For example, your dog may wake to find you home and give you that "where did you come from" or 'how did you sneak in without me hearing you" look.

Signs Your Dog is Partially Deaf

Depending on the cause, partial deafness or unilateral deafness can come with a wide range of symptoms or none at all.

Partial deafness as the result of an injury is often coupled with physical trauma that should be apparent. It's always a good idea to bring your dog to the vet if he experiences an injury, especially to the head.

Some dogs with build-up or an ear injury will scratch one ear more than the other. You may even notice your dog pawing one ear and slightly crying as he scratches. Dogs experiencing ear discomfort will also shake their heads.

Dogs that are deaf in one ear may favor one side more than another. What does this mean? They may approach you or another dog on an angle in order to better hear and respond. They may also sleep more deeply when one side of the head is pressed against their bed since their hearing ear is obstructed.

Signs Your Dog May Have Congenital Deafness

Deaf dogs do not come in a one-size-fits-all, but many demonstrate the same signs and symptoms that indicate they can't hear. For example, my dog is completely oblivious to hearing himself pass gas.

Some of the most common signs of congenital deafness include:

As a puppy

- Ignoring when littermates yelp or cry while playing.
- Not picking up on social cues from other dogs or their mother.
- Pigment deficiency.
- Sleeping more than littermates and not waking when others do.

At any age

- Ignoring you when you speak
- Ignoring sounds other dogs would respond to like doorbells, squeakers, and clickers.
- Sleeping deeply without waking to noise.
- Being easily startled by touch.
- Acting startled when waking up.
- A loud, awkward, tone-deaf bark.
- Intensely looking for visual cues or reacting strongly to visual movement.
- Barking at shadows or inanimate objects like stationary bikes, flags, and trash cans.

Signs I've Learned from Experience

Other, less common signs include dogs that let their ears be flipped the wrong way without noticing and/or displaying clinginess to their owners.

One obvious sign that Natchez is deaf is that he doesn't wake up when I get home. I often have to find him and wake him up. This odd behavior can be a little frightening when you first adopt your deaf dog since he can be asleep anywhere in your house and won't wake when you call him.

Also, deaf dogs don't react to "prey sounds" when on walks. What I mean by this is they don't hear the rustling in bushes and trees like normal dogs, so they often remain clueless to stimuli that would typically excite other dogs.

Finally, Natchez and many deaf dogs cannot fetch. My deafie can follow a ball if you roll it past him, but his lack of hearing makes it impossible to track where the ball goes once it leaves my hand and soars through the air.

Quick Home Tests

Is your dog's hearing cause for concern, or do you suspect your dog is losing his ability to hear? There are simple at-home tests you can perform. When I first brought Natchez home, I admit I didn't 100% believe he was completely deaf. I soon learned that my "tests" weren't accurate since deaf dogs can still feel vibrations, and some can pick up the highest register of sounds, too. Natchez can feel when my other dog barks, for example.

So, before you pull out the vacuum or blow a trumpet, try these. While these tests won't 100% prove your dog is deaf, they're a great indicator that it's time to ask your vet for a Brainstem Auditory Evoked Response Test (discussed further below).

Wake Up, Sleeping Beauty

This works best if your dog is in a deep sleep on a bed or location where the vibration of your footsteps won't wake him or her.

Slowly approach your dog from behind. Once you're within reach, clap your hands about three feet away from his ears. Don't clap too close because stirring the air may wake your dog.

Did your dog continue to slumber? If so, he may be deaf.

What Are You Squeaking About?

For this test, simply conceal a squeaker in your pocket or hide it beside you on your sofa. When your dog is calm and relaxed, slowly press the squeaker. The best squeakers for this experiment are not super high pitched. The ones that sound like a pig work really well.

No response from your dog? He may be deaf.

What Big Ears You Have!

I often make jokes about my deaf dog's ears like, "Look at how cute those useless ears are." He also often wakes up with what I call "bed ears" because they will be flipped inside out, and he doesn't bother fixing them right away. What does this have to do with testing your pooch for deafness? Well, dogs use their ears to locate where a sound is coming from. Deaf dogs do not.

Granted, deaf dogs will perk up their ears when they see their owners and at times act as if they're using them to hear, but most of this seems more about excitement than triangulating sound.

For this test, have a helper go into an adjacent room and whistle or make another noise. Have the helper take a few steps and repeat the whistle. If your dog does not turn his head in that direction or rotate his ears, this could be a sign of deafness.

The BAER Test

The Brainstem Auditory Evoked Response Test (or BAER test) is the diagnostic procedure vets use to confirm deafness in dogs. It's a neurological test, which means it looks at how the brain processes sound. This test detects unilateral deafness and bilateral deafness.

The BAER test measures and records electrical brain activity in areas that should respond to sound (the cochlea and auditory pathways). The vet places tiny electrodes under your dog's scalp right next to each ear, between his ears, and between the shoulder blades. Yes, this sounds painful, but most dogs barely notice the electrodes.

The vet will hold an earphone near your dog's ear. They will then hit play, and the earphone will play incremental clicking sounds as the electrodes record your dog's response. Each ear takes about 5 minutes to test.

The results look like a line graph with peaks when the dog can hear the click or a flattish line when their brain did not process the sound. Why "flattish"? Even dogs that are completely deaf frequently have minor peaks since they can feel the vibration on their skin and may slightly respond. After the test is complete, your vet can tell you whether your dog can hear and is unilaterally deaf or bilaterally deaf.

The BAER test is helpful beyond just getting a diagnosis for total deafness. It can indicate when your dog is partially deaf since the test reveals how well your dog can hear, and which ear has better hearing.

CHAPTER 2
Understanding Canine Deafness

What Causes Deafness in Dogs?

This question will cross your mind time and time again. I wish I had a straightforward answer, but the reality is that deafness in dogs can occur for myriad reasons. From injury to old age to genetics, your dog may not be able to hear, and you may never know exactly how your dog became deaf. Of course, if your sweet deafie is pigment deficient, he is likely a carrier of the piebald gene (which I will get into in this chapter).

As I've mentioned before, I get asked all the time, "Has Natchez always been deaf?" So, you may want to prepare to answer that question if you're adding a deaf dog to the family. You can always be a smart aleck and respond that all dogs are born deaf, which is true. Puppies are born with sealed ear canals, which open up within about two weeks.

There's also the follow-up question that usually comes along with it, "What caused his deafness?" While I usually respond that Natchez's deafness is caused by a genetic disorder, at times, I explain that it's likely caused by his double-merle coat.

This chapter is designed to provide you with a better understanding of how a dog's hearing works, the causes of congenital deafness, sudden onset deafness, and other causes of hearing loss. Hopefully, this will shine a light on why your dog is the unique and lovable dog that he is. You can then use that knowledge to teach other people when they ask questions.

Understanding How Hearing Works in Dogs

You've probably heard that dogs can hear better than we can. This is true. Hearing dogs can detect sounds more than twice as high pitched as we can (think: dog whistles). They can also detect sounds much softer than we can. This is why your dog knows you're almost home long before any human is in the house. Dogs aren't psychic; they just have super-ears.

What this means is that dogs have a finely tuned sense of hearing. And this ability has come in handy in terms of hunting and survival. Additionally, this means that a dog's ears do not work exactly the same way ours do. Although, in many ways, their hearing process is similar.

The Anatomy and Function of the Dog Ear

A dog's ear isn't just the soft adorable flap on each side of the head. Your dog has an outer ear, middle ear, and inner ear. The anatomy of your dog's ear is both similar and different from your own. Most of the elements are the same, but the shape and sizes are very different.

That "Fuzzy Flap" aka the Outer Ear

That fuzzy flap, nubs of cartilage, and ear canal make up the outer ear. The purpose of this part of the ear is to trap and route sound to the inner parts of the ear. Your dog's ear flap is called a "pinna."

HELPFUL TIP
Double J Dog Ranch

Situated in Hauser Lake, Idaho, the Double J Dog Ranch is a sanctuary and rehoming center for special-needs dogs serving the inland northwest area of the United States. This 501(c)3 organization offers training, specialized vet care, and a number of other services geared toward special-needs dogs. The organization was founded by Cristine Justus, who shares her 50-acre homestead with dogs who are at risk for euthanasia. As they say at the Double J Dog Ranch, "After all, they don't know they're any different...".

A dog's outer ear differs from a person's in that it's covered in fur, shaped like a triangle, and dogs have much deeper ear canals. Dogs also move their ears more easily than humans because they have eighteen ear muscles. This helps pinpoint where a sound is coming from.

The deeper ear canal works to concentrate sound better than a human's. While this isn't the perfect mental illustration, think of a long, narrow funnel versus a funnel that's squatter and has a wide opening for liquid to pour out of. Which type is going to allow for better accuracy and concentration? The longer, narrower funnel concentrates drops or a stream into a tighter formation.

Dogs with upright ears hear better than floppy-pinna-dogs. It makes sense, considering pointy ears look like satellite receivers.

The Middle Ear

A dog's ear canal starts at the outer ear and travels vertically before turning horizontally, toward the brain. This is where the middle ear begins.

The ear canal meets the tympanic membrane, also known as the eardrum. The eardrum looks like a dam between the ear canal and the tympanic chamber, an area filled with air and the three smallest bones in your dog's body. These tiny bones are often called the hammer, anvil, and stirrup. Their technical names are the malleus, incus, and stapes.

16

The three tiny bones in an ear direct and amplify sound toward the cochlea.

The middle ear has two tiny muscles, "an oval window" (the membrane covering the cochlea), and the auditory tube. The auditory tube actually connects the ear to the nose, so the tympanic chamber stays filled with air.

The Inner Ear

The inner ear is small but mighty. My favorite description of this unique structure is "the bony labyrinth," which is to say, it looks like a snail: hollow and concentric. The inner ear contains the cochlea and the vestibular system.

The cochlea twirls in tight circles. This organ has a thin membrane of hair cells that covers its internal walls. As sound bounces through the cochlea, the pressure of the sound is converted to electrochemical signals that are sent on to the brain and register as conscious sound.

The vestibular system is responsible for maintaining balance and helps with coordination. This system usually isn't affected in deaf dogs unless it's been physically injured.

Photo Courtesy of Peggy Leniger

What Exactly is Deafness?

Deafness is the inability to hear. When we refer to deafness, we usually mean total deafness, but deafness can also mean partial loss of hearing. This is why you'll hear and see some people refer to unilateral deafness or bilateral deafness. For the most part, I use deafness as a synonym for the total or majority loss or lack of hearing.

Deafness isn't always permanent, so some people modify the term as "temporary deafness." Ultimately, deafness is a breakdown somewhere along the path from the outer ear to the cochlea, where the sound is processed into signals for the brain. This means there are many parts, places, and causes for deafness in dogs.

Bilateral Deafness vs. Single Ear Deafness

Dogs can be partially deaf or completely deaf. When a dog cannot hear out of just one ear, it's called "unilateral deafness" or single-sided deafness. Unilateral deafness is more common for dogs.

Unilaterally deaf dogs can hear but cannot directionally locate sounds with their sense of hearing. It's kind of like how we lose depth perception when we close one eye. Many unilaterally deaf dogs will learn to compensate with their other senses. Many owners never realize their dogs are unilaterally deaf.

Unilateral deafness, like bilateral deafness, can be passed along from dogs to their puppies.

Bilateral deafness means that both ears lack the ability to process sounds. Of course, this means these dogs cannot track where a sound is coming from.

Bilateral deafies also learn to compensate for their lack of hearing, but not to the extent of unilateral deaf dogs (see: "They Heavily Rely on Their Other Senses").

Congenital Disorders

Congenital disorders can cause both unilateral and bilateral deafness. A congenital disorder simply means an abnormality that the dog was born with. Most congenital deafness is linked to genetics, which means it's often passed down from one or both parents. Most puppies that cannot hear have congenital deafness.

It's important to note that research into the cause of genetic deafness is ongoing. Most researchers agree that genetic deafness is often caused by dominant and/or recessive traits.

Double Merle and Coat Color

As discussed earlier, congenital deafness is most often linked to white pigmentation. This doesn't necessarily mean dog breeds that are lighter in color, like the Maltese or American Eskimo Dog, have higher rates of deafness. The white pigmentation in deaf dogs is actually a lack of pigmentation that their breed usually has. For example, a deaf Australian Shepherd may be all white. I prefer to refer to this as "pigment deficiency" because of this reason.

*Photo Courtesy
of Morgan Elizabeth*

Dog breeds with merle patterned coats have a higher percentage of deafness. The merle pattern is often recognized as patchy, mottled, and with lighter and darker spots of varying size. Dogs can be red merle, which means they have more browns and reds in their coat, while others are considered blue merles. Blue merles have blacks instead of browns or reds. The "merle" gene itself is responsible for the lighter areas of the coat. You can think of it as a bleaching effect, in a way.

When two merle dogs breed (no matter the breed, if they're red or blue), the result is a litter of merle and double-merle puppies. The double-merle puppies have two copies of the merle gene that appears twice, resulting in lighter coats (twice the bleaching effect).

For example, when a merle Great Dane mates with a merle Greyhound, their litter will likely be made up of 75% single merles and 25% double-merles. These double merle puppies are much more likely to also be deaf and pigment deficient.

One reason Dalmatians have such a high rate of deafness is they're considered extreme piebalds or merles, which is where they get their white coats and black spots. The duplication of the merle or "piebald allele" or piebald gene leads to a lack of pigmentation. How does this relate to a dog's ability to hear? Dogs typically have pigment-producing cells in their ears and eyes while they're developing before being born and after birth. Remember when I mentioned that all dogs are born deaf. This is true. And it's not until the second or third week of life that dogs that will remain deaf lose their physical ability to ever hear.

While scientists are still sorting things out, they believe the lack of pigmentation cells causes a restriction in blood supply and fluids to the cochlea. This causes the cochlea's nerve cells (those hair cells that pick up sound) to die. And without those nerve cells, sound cannot be transformed from pressure to electrochemical signals sent to the brain.

Double merles often have other health issues in addition to deafness, including abnormal pupils, sight issues, microphthalmia, sun sensitivity, and skin cancer (likely due to a lack of melanin).

Most Common Breeds with Congenital Deafness

Linking congenital deafness to specific breeds can be somewhat controversial. Many breeders and breed associations cover-up or, at least, don't disclose rates of congenital deafness out of fear that the breed or breeder will be seen as inferior. This becomes problematic when it comes to research since scientists have less opportunity to study how deafness presents in the full spectrum of breeds.

In fact, if you were to Google "how many dog breeds are reported to have deafness," you will see a wide range of answers from sources considered authorities. Some suggest 35 breeds, others 80 breeds, and some suggest 100 breeds. Dr. George M. Strain at Louisiana State University's School of

Veterinary Medicine has a list of over 104 instances of breeds with instances of congenital deafness.

That being said, some breeds have a reputation for higher rates of congenital deafness. My dog, Natchez, belongs to one: the Catahoula, a double-merle.

Some breeds with higher than average rates of deafness are:

Small Breeds

- Beagle
- Boston Terrier
- Mini Australian Shepherd
- Toy or Miniature Poodle
- Dachshund
- Maltese
- Cocker Spaniel
- French Bulldog
- Jack Russell Terrier
- Parson Russell Terrier
- West Highland Terrier

Medium Breeds

- Dalmatian
- Australian Cattle Dog
- English Bulldog
- Bull Terrier
- Shetland Terrier
- Akita
- English Setter
- Collie

Large Breeds

- Boxer
- Great Dane
- Australian Shepherd
- Pit Bull Terrier
- Catahoula Leopard Dog
- German Shepherd

Hearing Loss

When discussing deafness, congenital deafness is not the only form. There is also acquired deafness. Acquired deafness means that the dog became deaf at some point during its life, such as due to old age or injury.

If you notice your dog tilting his head, losing coordination, or having chronically itchy ears, take him to the vet.

Often, dogs with acquired hearing loss have better social skills but experience trouble when it comes to adapting to not being able to hear. Loss of hearing can cause stress, anxiety, depression, and disorientation for dogs.

If your dog loses his hearing, it's likely due to one of the following reasons.

Ear Infection or Otitis

Ear infections are the most common cause of acquired hearing loss. While one severe ear infection can cause deafness, so can having chronic ear infections over time. The inflammation causes both temporary hearing loss and damage to the ear.

The scab or build-up that comes along with an ear infection can also cause hearing loss.

Presbycusis or Hearing Loss as a Result of Old Age

As dogs and people get older, their hearing tends to go. One of the most common causes of deafness in senior dogs is a problem called "presbycusis." The middle part of the ear has three tiny bones that reflect sound onto the cochlea. As dogs get older, these bones get thicker, which makes them less effective.

Injury and Noise Trauma

Physical injury can cause temporary, permanent, unilateral, or bilateral deafness in dogs.

FUN FACT
Opal the Double Merle

Opal is a blind and deaf Australian Shepherd living in Spokane, Washington, with her owners, Christine Bray and Forrest Hutchings Bray. Opal gained internet celebrity status after a video of her welcoming her dad home from work went viral on Instagram. Now Opal and her dog sibling, Pearl, who is also deaf, have over twenty-one thousand followers on Instagram (@opalthedoublemerle). Opal is also the subject of the children's book bearing her name, written by her owner, Christine Bray, and illustrated by Anna Shawver.

These injuries are often caused by extremely loud noises and repetition of loud noises. The tiny muscles in the middle ear contract to become as tiny as possible in response to the loud noise. Over time the loud noises break down the hair cells in the cochlea, causing permanent hearing loss. Hunting dogs may experience this form of deafness caused by gunfire.

Physical injury can also result in damage to the ear or head, causing acquired deafness. Getting hit by a car would be one example of an extreme trauma that could cause deafness.

Tumors

Dogs can develop tumors in their ear canals. These tumors can spread and often need to be removed. The tumor itself or the treatment of removing the tumor can cause deafness.

You should check periodically for pink, purple, or white spots or growths in your dog's ears. These could be tumors.

Ototoxicity

Ototoxicity, or toxicity from chemicals or prescription drugs, can damage the inner ear permanently, resulting in deafness. When certain medicines or fluids are poured directly into the ear, they can penetrate the cochlea and destroy the hair cells.

Many of the prescription drugs and ear cleaning solutions that can cause deafness are no longer prescribed for ear infections or as cleaners.

Other Reasons

Some rarer causes and correlations for deafness in dogs include:

- General anesthesia (this is more common in senior dogs). Scientists aren't sure what causes this. They think the pushing of blood away from the cochlea or jaw compression could affect the cochlea.
- Obstruction: a dog can have something like a small stone or twig lodged in his ear canal.
- Build-Up: if a dog's ear wax builds up, it can cause temporary deafness.

CHAPTER 3

Understanding What Makes Deaf Dogs Unique

Deaf Dogs Are Special, Often in Lovely Ways

If you talk to anyone who's owned a deaf dog, they will likely tell you that their dog was one-of-a-kind. Deaf dogs exude quirky and unique personalities. From their attentive ability to memorize the smallest of their owners' habits and routines to wanting to please their owners, deafies tend to have classic dog behaviors, but magnified, while other typical dog tendencies are absent.

Deaf dogs remain individuals, while exhibiting common personality traits they share with other deafies. While deafness is often considered a limitation, it molds many dogs into snuggle-bugs that intently watch their owners while awaiting hand signals and to find out their next move.

In this chapter, you'll learn about the distinct challenges and gifts that make deaf dogs one-of-a-kind canine companions.

They Can Be Trained

All dogs need discipline and training to become civil and obedient family dogs. The same is true of deafies. Deaf dogs can and do thrive when their owners set behavioral expectations and consistently work with them.

FUN FACT
Deaf Dog Awareness Week

Deaf Dog Awareness Week falls on the last full week of September every year. Though deaf dogs are always worthy of celebration, this is a great week to spread awareness of the unique and special qualities of these canines or to make a donation to your local Humane Society.

Unlike hearing dogs, deaf dogs rely only on their eyesight to translate hand signals into the desired behavior. When observing most deaf dogs, you may notice that they often cock their heads while intently staring at their owners' hands, awaiting a command. Their focus is often intense and unbreakable.

They also learn very quickly from other dogs, glancing to

see how their brothers or sisters react to a command and then mimicking the behavior.

They Want to Learn

Many people are surprised to learn that my deaf dog was easier to train than my hearing dog. Why was this? While I cannot be 100% sure, I believe it's because his lack of hearing eliminates distractions and increases his desire to please.

When I first adopted Natchez, he was the only dog in my home. He was also extremely food motivated (likely because of being deprived of nutrition before his life with me). While his food motivation created some problems like foraging through the trash and trying to get on the counter, it also made it easy for me to get him to focus on training treats.

I can clearly remember his excitement when it clicked that my signal for "sit" meant 'put my butt on the floor, and I'll get a treat.' The connection between my hand signal, his sitting, and the treat only took him a few minutes, and the impact has lasted a lifetime. Natchez could not contain his excitement for performing this simple task. He'd stand, then sit, then stand, then sit, over and over again.

He still reflexively will sit when he wants to impress or remind me that he's a good boy. Natchez reliably also does his commands more promptly and with less confusion than his hearing brother.

Natchez's learning this command prompted a major change in his personality and behavior. The realization that we could communicate seemed to provide him with reassurance and purpose. After learning to sit, he continued (and continues now) to excel at learning. In fact, by the time we arrived at his first day of doggie school, he had mastered most of the commands they covered.

Whenever I can, I foster deaf dogs, teaching them to sit as quickly as possible. I've always found that they pick up the behavior rapidly and learn in a similar way as hearing dogs.

They Heavily Rely on Their Other Senses

Deaf dogs are highly reliant on their remaining senses. Additionally, it makes their mannerisms different from dogs that can hear.

If you choose to adopt a deafie, one thing that never fails is even after explaining that your dog is deaf, people will still talk to your dog, make kissy noises, whistle, snap, and even clap as if your dog can hear them. And while this often makes them feel silly, I reassure them that the friendly body

language is still appreciated by deaf dogs. And this is true. Deaf dogs take note of facial expressions, hand gestures, and postures. My husband and I both verbally talk to our deaf dog while signing commands, greeting him, or whatever feels natural. In fact, your deaf dog may come up with some signs of their own that naturally occur as you interact: waving bye, for example.

As friends and family verbally try to call Natchez, I am always reminded that as people, our first instinct is to try to communicate with dogs audibly. This is because the majority of human communication is verbal, and experience has taught us that dogs have highly acute senses of hearing.

Think about it: a loose dog is running along on a sidewalk. You want to catch this dog to return her to her owner. What's your first response? To call after her, right? We would likely think the dog is strange if she didn't slow down and turn her head in the direction of the voice. Over time, we've been conditioned to expect dogs to react to our voices. When they don't, it can catch some people off-guard. This unexpected lack of reaction can make deaf dogs seem odd at times, especially if you're on a walk, and your deaf dog ignores a stranger trying to get the dog's attention. This, combined with a deaf dog's odd bark, can elicit some odd responses and looks.

Because they don't react like normal dogs, deafies may seem peculiar to some people. For example, Natchez loves to come in my front door, so he will jog from the back of the house to the front. If anyone is around, it probably seems very odd that I don't just call his name. Instead, I have to chase after him to touch him to get him to turn around. Odd? Yup. Frustrating at times? Of course. Can this quirk be fixed? Vibration training can replace verbal recall for most deaf dogs. If you want to learn more about vibration training, see chapter 7.

Other Senses

I'm sure you've probably heard the adage that when a person is blind or deaf, their other senses become keener. Well, studies have proven this to also be true when it comes to deaf dogs.[1] It's not that a deaf dog has a better sense of smell; it's that when the brain doesn't create connections between the ears, sound, hearing, and interpreting hearing, the brain creates and strengthens other avenues to better interpret signals from the other senses. It's more of a brain adaptation than a change in the ability to sense.

Furthermore, deaf dogs seem to maintain some of the sensing systems present at puppyhood before their eyes and ears open. When puppies are

---

1   Stephen G. Lomber, M. Alex Meredith and Andrej Kral, "Cross-modal Plasticity in Specific Auditory Cortices Underlies Visual Compensations in the Deaf," Nature Neuroscience 13, no. 11 (2010):1421-7. https://doi.org/10.1038/nn.2653.

born, their ears and eyes are sealed closed. This leaves them more reliant on other means of sensation to explore and navigate the world. Puppies can smell where their moms are and head that way. They can also feel her warmth and know they're safe. Studies suggest while hearing dogs become desensitized to these, deaf dogs home in more on these forms of detection.

So, deaf dogs rely more heavily on their whiskers, vibration sensation, temperature sensation, and internal ability to feel changes in pressure.

For many decades, experts have been fascinated by the fact that some deafies act as if they can hear. For example, some deaf dogs seemingly sense other dogs barking without being able to see them bark. How can they know their sibling is barking without being able to hear? Scientists have suggested this is most likely due to vibration sensing and a change in pressure in the room. If you want to go one step further, there is the possibility that the deaf dog smells the nervous pheromones related to barking or smells the other dog's breath.

Deaf dogs also use their humans and dog siblings as an extension of their senses. "Velcroing," which I will devote more time to in this chapter, is often recognized as an adaptation. While your deaf dog is asleep, he or she will likely want to be in physical contact with you so that he'll know when you get up.

When discussing a dog's hierarchy of senses, it's vital to understand that dogs rely more heavily on their sense of sight and smell than their sense of hearing. Of course, not being able to hear is a disadvantage, but it is not a fatal handicap. When it comes to communication, dogs more often perceive and express their thoughts and feelings non-verbally, through body language, compared to how humans communicate. This is likely because body language was more effective when hunting in packs. This means that deaf dogs can often function as upstanding dog citizens when playing and interacting with others.

A Deaf Dog's Sense of Sight

When it comes to their sense of sight, dogs have better peripheral vision than humans, but the acuteness of their vision is not as refined. Dogs that are born deaf adapt to relying on their eyesight more than a typical dog. One sense many experts believe deaf dogs retain from puppyhood is their ability to see infrared light.[2]

Peripheral vision often comes in handy with a deaf dog. If you want to get a deaf dog's attention, waving is a great way to accomplish this. Natchez

---

2   Stanley Coren, How Dogs Think: Understanding the Canine Mind (New York: Free Press, 2004).

seems to distinguish slight changes in light better than his hearing brother. If he wants to sleep deeply, he'll tuck himself under a blanket. But if I'm not home, a shadow passing over his closed eyes will often wake him.

Sense of Smell

Dogs have much more sophisticated senses of smell than we do. Not only do they detect minuscule smells, but they can separate smells from one another more easily. For example, we smell trash, while our dogs can smell eggshells, banana peels, and whatever else was tossed in the bin.

Dogs also rely on their noses for navigation. This is often referred to as "olfactory mapping," and it came in extremely handy for wild dog packs when hunting and traveling at night. Domesticated dogs still use scents to detect visitors and changes in their environment.

As for deafies, their sense of smell becomes one of the main ways they learn about the world and changes to their environment. Some deaf dog owners remark that their dog can tell they arrived home because they smelled them enter the house or the waft of fresh air from the opening of the door.

I often credit Natchez's sharp sense of smell with how easy he was to train. While deaf dogs aren't born with better senses of smell, their need to rely on their other senses makes them more attuned to their surroundings.

If you want to have some fun with your deaf dog, scent training games can be a blast. Try hiding treats around your living room or house and watching your deafie hunt them out.

Feeling It Out: A Deaf Dog's Keen Sense of Touch

The sense of touch becomes vital to deaf dogs and how they communicate with their owners. Often, tapping your deaf dog is the easiest way to get his or her attention. With tap-training, your deaf dog will also learn that touching you with his or her nose is a way to communicate.

Deaf dogs also seem very adept at feeling wind or "air-motion," changes in temperature, and changes in air pressure. Every now and then, I catch Natchez looking up and around and then barking at the vents. Most dogs seem to be able to sense changes in barometric pressure, which alerts them to seek cover before storms.

Deaf dogs also rely on vibration sensing. It makes sense that most hearing dogs become desensitized to feeling minor vibrations, senses that can get overstimulated by all the input they have available to them. In my observation, it seems as if hearing dogs tend to ignore vibrations, while deaf dogs become more and more in-tune with them over time.

Natchez can often feel the vibrations in the floor from someone walking. He can also feel the air motion and vibrations from a door opening and closing.

They Love to Snuggle

Deaf dogs are the definition of "Velcro dogs." They are constantly attached to their owners. If you're looking for a dog that likes to snuggle or cuddle, there's an excellent chance your deafie will surpass your expectations.

Annoying Quirks

Owning a deaf dog offers more gratification than I could ever truly describe, but it's not all roses and cake. Natchez, like so many other deaf dogs, has some quirks that I could live without. Of course, I feel the benefits of deaf dog ownership far outweigh these, but that may not be the same for everyone.

Barking

Deaf dogs typically have very loud barks since they never learn to modulate their voices to fit the room or severity of the situation. They often sound tone-deaf, monotone, or just plain weird. Some deaf dogs have very high-pitched barks, while others have low graveling voices. I fostered one deaf Bull Terrier puppy that sounded like a squeak toy.

FUN FACT

Deaf Dog Education Action Fund (DDEAF)

DDEAF was founded in 1996 by members of a deaf dogs email list, who were attempting to raise money to transport deaf dogs to loving homes and avoid shelters where the animals could be euthanized. The mission of DDEAF is "to provide education and funding for the purpose of improving and/or saving the lives of deaf dogs." The organization is a 501(c)(3) nonprofit and relies on donations and membership fees to operate.

I've noticed other people are often startled by how loud Natchez's bark is. Sometimes he sounds like he's barking through a megaphone. This can be intimidating to new friends.

Most deaf dogs also bark at times when hearing dogs may not. For example, many deaf dogs love to bark as they play. Natchez, like many deaf dogs, will bark while running and chasing other dogs at the dog park. Again, fellow dog owners will often give us funny looks. Some people even get nervous or scared because his bark is so 'big.'

What Makes Deaf Dogs Bark?

It's easy to understand what makes hearing dogs bark. It's often sound: the doorbell, the car door, voices passing by the house. That isn't the case when it comes to deaf dogs, although some of the motivation is the same.

Joy and excitement are two unexpected reasons deaf dogs may bark. As I explained, many deafies bark while playing with other dogs. The reaction from their peers may positively reinforce the barking, or the vibrations simply feel good. Of course, it may be the case that many hearing dogs try barking while playing at some point and just realize that it's not effective or appreciated by other pups.

Natchez likes to literally scream with joy when he gets leashed for a walk. The sound he makes is very similar to the sound a dog might make if you step on his or her tail. He makes a slightly less screeching sound when he realizes he's going on a car ride (his favorite activity in the world).

Stress and anxiety are two other reasons that fall on the other end of the spectrum from fun and joy. Anxiety-induced barking can be the result of feeling vulnerable, intimidated, uncertain, or unconfident.

To decide if your deaf dog is barking as a result of anxiety, pay attention to your dog's body language and the context of the barking. When Natchez is barking because of anxiety, he often won't make eye contact with whatever it is that he's afraid of. Other signs of stress include panting, stiff limbs, inability to relax or settle, shaking, pacing, hiding, and accidental urination. If you notice these, it's often best to contact a behaviorist (see Chapter 6), but exercise and mental stimulation can help ease a deaf dog's anxiety.

Some deaf dogs bark due to separation anxiety. These barks, whimpers, and cries can be positively heartbreaking. Natchez used to suffer from separation anxiety, and he'd let out a very sad, high-pitched whine as I shut the door. There were also times I would get home, and he'd be on the bed, still whimpering and crying in a low, muffled voice.

Frustration can trigger barking for some deaf dogs. If Natchez's dinner is taking too long, or he's confused about a command, he will bark. Unfortunately, because deaf dogs have such sonically impactful barks, they learn that this method is excellent for getting their owners to pay attention, react, and respond in a way to get the barking to stop.

This causes inadvertent reinforcement. I learned this the hard way. Natchez greets guests in our home by barking. Naturally, I believed this was a sign of nervousness and anxiety at having strangers in the home. I began having guests try to gain his trust with treats. Eventually, he would bark and then get a treat. He connected these actions in his mind, thinking that barking at houseguests was an easy method to earn treats. It took sessions with a behaviorist to learn this, and even so, Natchez still falls back into this habit.

Some deaf dogs will bark when they're confused. If Natchez thinks I'm putting my shoes on to go on a walk, he will bark out of excitement. He will also bark if he thinks I'm going to answer the door, even if I'm not. This type of barking can, in turn, confuse deaf dog owners since it can be hard to determine which of your actions, daily rituals, or routines your deaf dog has memorized.

Many deaf dog parents have had luck modifying the behavior to minimize the barking. The key to success is being able to identify exactly what triggers your deaf dog to bark and replacing the negative with positive reinforcement. Other deaf dog owners struggle to train their deaf dogs to stop barking. Natchez's success waxes and wanes in this department.

Citronella Anti-Barking Collars

Most anti-bark products are designed for hearing dogs. Some work for deafies, too. Several companies make Citronella anti-bark collars, which spray a light mist of citrus scent when the dog barks. Dogs naturally dislike this smell, creating a negative association with barking. These are hit or miss with deaf dogs, though. They work great for some, but not all.

There are a few downsides to this product. The first is that the barking of other dogs can trigger the spray sometimes. Non-barking vibrations can trigger the spray as well.

Another downside is the sound detection and spray box on these collars is quite bulky. The box is about the size of a ring box, which looks ridiculous on a small dog. Also, because they are one-size-fits-all, some dog owners remark that the spray is either too direct or lands directly under the dog's chin, not really affecting the dog at all.

Natchez used to wear a Citronella anti-barking collar. I always felt a little embarrassed that the collar looked like a shock-collar. I assumed people either thought I was cold-hearted or Natchez was vicious. I also remember feeling like an awful dog owner when I forgot to switch it off, and he stuck his head out of the car window, and the wind triggered the spray. He was sprayed continually until I could pull over and switch the collar off.

Ultimately, his collar stopped working after he wore it while running through too many puddles.

The collar did help a bit. Natchez learned to bark more softly, almost silently, so as not to trigger the spray. If your deaf dog barks a lot, I would say the collar is worth a try. They usually run about forty dollars, with refills for the spray costing about fifteen.

Ultrasonic Collars and Devices

Ultrasonic collars and devices are one of the latest technologies to discourage barking. These work by using sound that is at the highest range of a dog's hearing, making it silent to people. The sound works similarly to a dog whistle.

Does it work for deaf dogs? Unilaterally deaf dogs will be able to hear the sound, although dogs that are bilaterally deaf most often do not. As I explained earlier, some dogs born bilaterally deaf do retain the ability to hear the highest register of sound. Still, every review I've read suggests these don't work for deaf dogs, making them a waste of your time and money.

The exception to the rule would be if your companion dog reacts to the door, mailman, or passersby, triggering your deaf dog to bark. If this is the case, the ultrasonic anti-bark device may be a great investment. If you stop the hearing dog from barking, you stop the deaf dog from joining in.

Training a Deaf Dog not to Bark

Training a deaf dog to not bark is the most consistent and surefire way to eliminate unnecessary barking. There are different methods, depending on what triggers your deaf dog's barking. This section works best when paired with Chapter 5.

How to Train Your Deaf Dog to Reduce or Eliminate Frustration Barking

When retraining your deaf dog's brain, the first thing to remember is that rewarding your dog for barking will worsen the problem.

When your dog barks at you because he or she is impatient, ignore the behavior until the barking stops. For that brief moment, reward the dog and give your "clicker" sign. If your dog begins barking again, repeat.

If your dog is frustration-barking from a situation that doesn't occur often, like something blocking the path or your dog is trying to figure out a treat puzzle, you're probably better off just leaving your dog alone. If you want the barking to stop, you can distract your dog and remove the trigger.

Barking for Fun and Joy

There's not a whole lot you can do about this since your dog is likely so distracted and stimulated that he will ignore whatever signal you may give. If you use a vibration collar, it may work. If your dog ignores it, do not keep pressing the button, as you will desensitize your dog to its effect.

Barking from Anxiety

First and foremost, if your deaf dog has extreme anxiety, you may want to consult your veterinarian or a veterinary behaviorist (as opposed to a typical behaviorist). Your dog may benefit from a prescription. Often, if you let anxiety symptoms and barking go unchecked, your dog's behavior will worsen.

Most behaviorists will recommend desensitization and replacing the negative feelings towards the trigger with positive ones through positive reinforcement. The "look at that command" is what I used with Natchez. When he's feeling anxious, but the trigger is still far away, he will look at what's causing his anxiety and then check-in with me. Immediately after checking in, he earns a treat. This redirects his attention and behavior, occupying him with a positive and wanted behavior instead of barking.

You can also expose your dog to whatever he barks at. Wait for a moment, and as soon as the barking stops, 'click' sign and reward your dog. This can be done in sessions that progressively get longer.

Photo Courtesy of Julia Philp

Separation Anxiety

All dogs can develop separation anxiety. If your dog tends to show signs of anxiety or sulking as you get ready to leave, he or she may be experiencing separation anxiety. The most common signs of separation anxiety in dogs include destructive behavior when left alone, like chewing, crying, scratching at the door, trying to escape when you leave, having accidents when you leave, or howling.

It's believed that deaf dogs may develop separation anxiety more frequently than hearing dogs. While there currently are not any studies that compare the frequency of cases between hearing dogs and non-hearing dogs, many deaf dog owners report that their dogs have suffered from separation anxiety at some point.

The cause of separation anxiety in dogs, hearing and non-hearing, has yet to be fully understood by scientists. In fact, many studies show contradictory results as to what predisposes some dogs to distressed behavior when their owners depart.[3] The main triggers for separation anxiety often involve a major change to a dog's schedule, routine, or home. These changes can destabilize a dog's sense of comfort and normality, leaving them uncertain of their safety, future, and wellbeing. And dogs that exhibit more attachment to their owners tend to be more susceptible to separation anxiety. Additionally, dogs adopted from shelters are more likely to have separation anxiety than those adopted from a litter of a family member or friend. Deaf dogs are more often obtained from shelters and rescues rather than from breeders or family friends.

Despite not having definite answers regarding why deaf dogs sometimes suffer from separation anxiety, there are many valid reasons for deaf dogs to feel panicky and nervous when left alone. First, their inability to hear leaves them more vulnerable, which may be a source of nervousness. In addition to vulnerability, deaf dogs come to rely on their owners for pointers and cues. When their owners are away, they may feel handicapped.

It's also important to remember that deaf dogs, along with all recently adopted hearing dogs, often go through a phase of separation anxiety, which often diminishes on its own. This phase may not occur immediately after adoption. It may take a week or a few weeks to develop since your dog will be developing trust, reliance, and see you as a sense of security.

---

3   Rebecca J. Sargisson, "Canine Separation Anxiety: Strategies for Treatment and Management," Veterinary Medicine: Research and Reports, no. 5 (2014): 143-151, https://www.dove-press.com/front_end/cr_data/cache/pdf/download_1608571084_5fe0d8cc37d7e/VMRR-60424-canine-separation-anxiety--strategies-for-treatment-and-mana_103014.pdf.

When I adopted Natchez, he had a really bad case of separation anxiety for the first week. He tore his dog bed to ribbons, and he managed to pry the metal bars of his crate apart. Needless to say, it was intense. Then it faded after I moved his crate to the front room, where he could relax in his crate and still feel like we were together. He could also see me leave. He developed another case of separation anxiety after we moved from Louisiana to Florida and from Florida to Tennessee. These incidents are typical scenarios where separation anxiety could crop up, and luckily, he adjusted to the change, and his anxiety went away.

How to Help Your Dog Cope with Separation

As a dog owner, separation anxiety can be heart-wrenching. The emotions and guilt of leaving your dog can be overwhelming, especially if your dog scrambles to get out the door and cries. When a dog expresses anxiety through destruction, pet owners often feel an added layer of dread as they worry about what they'll find in shreds when they arrive home. It's important to check in with yourself and remind yourself that your dog is okay, and he can overcome separation anxiety. If you feel overwhelmed or your dog's anxiety is severe, contact a behaviorist or your veterinarian. Otherwise, you can try some of the tactics described below to help your dog better cope when you leave.

If your deaf dog has separation anxiety, do not punish your dog for destructive behavior. This has been shown to actually increase the dog's anxiety.[4]

If your dog is crated, moving the crate to an area of the house where your dog can see you exit can help. Deaf dogs cannot hear the door open, so your disappearance can be more confusing if they believe you may be somewhere in the house. Some deaf dog owners try sneaking out of the house without their dog knowing they're leaving. This can increase anxiety after the fact and destabilize your dog's ability to learn that exiting through the door means you're temporarily leaving.

Desensitization

Desensitization is often cited as the most successful method to help reduce and eliminate separation anxiety. This method, through incremental exposure, helps your dog learn that your leaving is ok and only temporary.

If your deaf dog has memorized your movements leading up to leaving and begins to express signs of separation anxiety, then you'll want to start there. Try to spend as much time as you can during your first desensitization

---

4   Rebecca Sargisson,. "Canine separation anxiety."

training. Take breaks to help your dog recuperate, rest, and mentally reset. But if you can get through your entire leaving routine without actually needing to leave for an extended period of time, your dog will be less apt to backstep.

Isolate which of your actions causes the anxiety to start: putting your shoes on, walking toward the front door, grabbing your keys and coat. Perform this action in sight of your deaf dog, but do not leave. Return to your normal activities around the house. As difficult as it may be, ignore your dog's cries. Comforting your dog can reinforce the behavior. Stay calm, and your dog will calm down. Repeat this until your dog's anxiety lessens.

After your dog's anxiety lessens over the initial trigger, you can graduate to exiting the door. You can help your dog feel more confident and in control by having him sit and stay several feet away from the door. Toss your dog a treat. Of course, if you recently adopted your dog, you may not be at this point. If this is the case, I would recommend looking over the crate training section in chapter 5.

Once your dog is sitting and staying, open the door and exit. Stay on the other side of the door for a few seconds, then come back through. Repeat this and lengthen the amount of time you are away. After your dog seems to be adjusting to you disappearing outside, you can practice your full leaving routine.

Give your dog time. If you get overwhelmed, take a break. Try to practice this every day.

Medication and Pheromones

It's always a good idea to stay in contact with your vet about your dog's behavior. Your vet can advise you if your dog is a good candidate for a prescription to help manage anxiety.

Many dog owners who are looking for an alternative to prescriptions choose to try pheromone options before medications. Unlike prescriptions, pheromone therapy doesn't come with side effects and can be easier to use (you don't have to trick your dog into swallowing a pill). You can find pheromone products through your vet or over the counter that can help calm your dog. Adaptil is one of the most popular pheromone products for dogs.

Like many products designed for pets, pheromones don't work for all dogs. But studies show that pheromones do effectively calm most dogs and reduce symptoms of anxiety.[5]

---

5   Young-Mee Kim et al., "Efficacy of Dog-appeasing Pheromone (DAP) for Ameliorating Separation-related Behavioral Signs in Hospitalized Dogs." The Canadian Veterinary Journal 51, no. 4, (2010):380-384.

Pheromones are chemicals that interact with areas of the brain to produce different effects. There are natural pheromones that light up certain areas of a dog's brain. For example, a mother dog will produce a pheromone called the "dog appeasing pheromone" that calms and comforts puppies. Pheromone diffusers and collars contain synthetic versions of these chemicals that identically mimic the natural pheromones. When a dog smells these pheromones, an organ called the Jacobson's organ, which is in the roof of the mouth, takes these scents in and sends signals to areas of the brain that are stimulated and produce a calming effect for a dog.

The diffusers have a limited range, while the collars do not. Most of the refills and collars last about four weeks. These can also work well in combination with desensitization training.

In addition to medications and pheromones, there is one new medical device available to help deaf dogs overcome and reduce their anxiety: the Calmer Canine halo. This is an Assisi Loop that dogs wear for two fifteen minutes sessions daily for four to six weeks. It uses targeted pulsed electromagnetic field (tPEMF) technology to work on a cellular level by sending electromagnetic signals to the part of the brain responsible for anxiety. Pilot studies have shown that the majority of dogs that use the Calmer Canine device show improvement.

I discovered this device by chance while writing about how it helps pets with postoperative recovery. Their website had a tiny section at the time that said they were testing its effectiveness on helping dogs with anxiety. I was skeptical, of course, but after talking to my veterinarian, I decided to try Calmer Canine to see if it could help Natchez with his clinginess and separation anxiety symptoms. To my surprise, Natchez did become less anxious and nervous over time. Natchez loved wearing it. He would wag his tail and practically dive into the harness. As for results, he began choosing to sleep on his bed and became more content, not clinging to me. While the use of tPEMF for separation anxiety is relatively new, it does offer long-lasting improvement for dogs without the use of prescription drugs.

Exercise, Training, and Mental Stimulation

Staying busy, engaged, and mentally stimulated is beneficial to all dogs. Exercise and mental stimulation lead to more restful sleep and reduced anxiety.[6] Dogs with separation anxiety can release some nervous energy and gain purpose and confidence through exercise and training.

Studies show that dogs that are exposed to more situations outside of the home as puppies have lower rates of separation anxiety. This is likely

---

6   Sargisson, "Canine Separation Anxiety."

due to gained confidence and independence in addition to developing a less fearful attitude. Exercise and mental stimulation also reduce boredom, which can lead to destructive behavior.

You can help your deaf dog through daily training, scent games, walks, treat puzzles, dog park trips, and interactive toys.

A Sibling

Deaf dogs with canine siblings often cope with separation better than only-dogs. Because deaf dogs rely on their owners for cues about the world around them, they can feel more deprived and nervous when their owners are away. If they can receive these cues from another dog, the fear of being alone and vulnerable is reduced.

So, should you adopt another dog? It's a huge decision that I discuss in chapter 6.

The Assisi Loop and Targeted Pulsed Electromagnetic Field Technology

Targeted Pulsed Electromagnetic Field Technology (tPEMF) has been shown to help dogs with separation anxiety.[7] These devices work by pulsing electrical currents to your dog's brain, reducing inflammation, realigning neurons, and increasing the body's natural production of nitric oxide to help the brain function better and achieve a calm state more easily. Dogs do not feel the current. The device for separation anxiety looks like a little halo attached to a vest. The dog wears the vest for one session of tPEMF each day for a few months.

As of 2020, this technology is relatively new when it comes to treating dog separation anxiety. I suspect there will be more products developed at lower prices in the near future. While the clinical studies show tPEMF to be effective in reducing separation anxiety (not completely eliminating it), the device is a financial investment.

Shadow Barking and Chasing

While shadow barking and chasing are not behaviors limited to deaf dogs, these ticks do seem to pop up frequently for deafies. Most sources suggest that chasing shadows and lights is a form of canine Obsessive-Compulsive Disorder (OCD), but when it comes to deaf dogs, especially those with some

---

7   Natalie Zidan et al., "The Effect of Electromagnetic Fields on Post-Operative Pain and Locomotor Recovery in Dogs with Acute, Severe Thoracolumbar Intervertebral Disc Extrusion: A Randomized, Placebo Controlled Prospective Clinical Trial, Journal of Neurotrauma 35, no. 15 (August 2018)::1726-1736. https://doi.org/10.1089/neu.2017.5485.

vision impairment, they do not realize that shadows are inanimate because they don't make sounds.

We, as people, recognize that shadows are not alive and are connected to the object that is casting them onto a surface. We learn this through observation. We see that the shadow syncs up with movement and does not project any sound. If you think about how a deaf dog sees the world, shadows become foreign, frightening, and confusing.

Here's one example that I think illustrates this well: When I first adopted Natchez, we'd go on walks at night through a field that bordered an apartment building and a Walgreens. The lights that lit up the parking lots projected our shadows onto a dumpster about 50 feet away. These shadows were narrow but tall. Seeing these terrifying, dark figures caused Natchez to startle, lunge backward, then bark in their direction. How was he to know they were simply a projected figure where we blocked the light? How was he to know they were harmless and not moving toward us? Without the ability to hear, these everyday occurrences can be very scary. Over time, deaf dogs will learn that shadows like these are harmless, but you can anticipate situations like this every now and then.

I also remember a predicament, when out of nowhere, Natchez discovered that ceiling fans cast shadows on the ceiling. He'd look up at the ceiling, hunker down, and bark. It took about a week for me to figure out what the problem was. The movement in light, combined with the movement of air, made the fan seem 'alive' or at least intimidating to him. When the fan wasn't running, Natchez was fine. I went a week or so with no ceiling fans. When I turned them back on, he was fine.

Natchez was also very confused by a space heater. Between the temperature and glowing coils, it must have been very confusing to him. As a deaf dog owner, you can expect these mysteries to come up from time to time.

As for shadow chasing or light chasing, you should avoid using a flashlight or laser pointer as a toy. If you decide later on to use flashlight signals or a laser pointer as your 'clicker,' the play-instinct can set you up for failure.

If you notice your deaf dog wanting to chase shadows, discourage the behavior through redirection. Be sure your dog is receiving plenty of mental stimulation, play, and exercise, and check with your vet to see if a dietary supplement could help. The idea is that you do not want this behavior to become compulsory. You want your dog to be able to ignore shadows to the best of his or her ability. If your deaf dog does verge into the OCD realm, it can be mentally distressing for the dog and a preoccupation that doesn't allow for psychological downtime or relief.

Nervousness and Self-Confidence

Many deaf dogs can come across as nervous. This nervousness or lack of self-esteem can manifest in negative ways like barking and lunging. If you've ever witnessed an injured dog show his teeth, snarl, and snap, you know that this dog is trying to protect himself. The same can be said for some nervous deaf dogs—they may present aggressive warning signs as a way to appear more confident. Other dogs will appear anxious in more typical ways: tail tucking, hiding, cowering, and avoid eye contact.

These tendencies can be overcome.

A lot of nervous behaviors come from feeling scared or frightened of the world. Slow exposure to other dogs, places, and scenarios can help a dog build confidence and understanding.

Training and dog classes also do a lot to help deaf dogs feel more confident. As your deaf dog learns that you can communicate with him or her, your dog will begin to feel more secure with having his or her needs met. Learning commands also helps a dog feel more independent in their skills.

Getting assistance with a trainer can also help you and your dog navigate the world with your heads held high.

Velcro-Dog

Deaf dogs are Velcro-dogs. There's no other way to put it. They cling to their owners, siblings, and often house guests. As I noted earlier, deaf dog owners become an extension or sensing tool for their deaf dogs. This means that if you're home, you can expect your deaf dog to want to be in the same room as you and probably have some form of physical contact with you.

Your deaf dog will likely learn to not being directly under-foot, but it can take a little time. You may accidentally step on some toes, but that's part of the process.

Natchez will lie beside the bathtub during showers. He will also lie against any door that separates us. I suspect if his sibling, Fritz, was more receptive to it, he would cling more to him. Many deaf dog owners that I've spoken with say that their deafies tend to hang with their siblings more than them.

As a dog owner, you have to decide where to draw the line: sleeping in bed with you, sitting on your ottoman. Just know that deaf dogs are naturally very attached to their caretakers. If this is not a characteristic you appreciate, you may not want to adopt a deafie.

CHAPTER 4
Choosing to Adopt a Deaf Dog

What to Consider When Deciding

Adding a new dog to your life is a major decision. A dog is dependent on its owner for all necessary care. This can put immense pressure on you as you decide on your next canine companion. The pressure of deciding can translate into worry, uncertainty, self-doubt, and guilt as you scroll through website after website of dogs in need of loving families.

When it comes to deciding on potentially adopting a deaf dog, all of the pressure can be coupled with the fear of the unknown. Most potential deaf dog adopters haven't spent very much time with deaf dogs, and even fewer have raised one. Websites can leave you reeling with confusion; some say it's no different than caring for a hearing dog, while other websites make caring for a deaf dog sound like you need eight arms and a certificate in dog behavior.

The reality is deaf dogs can require a bit more consideration when it comes to training, but for the most part, the additional consideration is more of a change in mindset rather than a time investment.

If you feel intimidated by the idea of adopting a deaf dog, that's normal. Just know that anyone capable of caring for a dog is capable of providing a deaf dog everything they need and want.

When it comes to time and cost, the only major investment you may need to consider is whether your dog would benefit from a behaviorist. Additionally, all dogs, especially deafies, benefit from socialization with other people and dogs. These considerations apply to many different types of dogs, though.

FUN FACT
Ghost

Ghost is a narcotic K-9 with the Washington State Department of Social and Health Services, and he also happens to be deaf. Ghost, formerly known as Gator, was rescued in Florida, but due in part to his deafness, he was placed on a euthanasia list. Luckily, Ghost was rehomed to the Olympic Peninsula Humane Society in Washington State, where Dr. Suzy Zustiak connected the energetic pup with an experienced narcotic K-9 trainer, Barbara Davenport. Ghost completed a 240-hour course with his current handler, Joe Henderson, who communicates with Ghost via hand signals and a vibrating collar.

One question you will want to ask yourself is why you're adopting a dog. If you want a dog to play fetch with or a hunting buddy, a deaf dog isn't the right choice. If you want a dog that will sleep soundly, make you laugh, and return your kindness with love, consider adopting a deaf dog.

Will Your Personality Mesh Well with a Deaf Dog's?

Like all dogs, deafies are individuals, each with his own personality. So, the easiest way to decide if a deaf dog is the right choice for you is to spend some time with it. All dogs take time to house train and get acclimated to your routine. If you don't have time for training a dog, I would suggest adopting a lower-maintenance pet.

One of the best ways to determine whether you're cut out for a deaf dog is to foster one or volunteer at a shelter that takes in deafies. Most people, once they've been around deaf dogs, realize that deafies are not all that different from hearing dogs. They will chase you, lick you, wag their tails, and happily play with other dogs. Talking to the staff at a shelter can also help you get a better idea of an individual dog's personality.

Whether you're laid back or type-A, deaf dogs make great companions. Type-A people tend to love the training involved in owning deaf dogs. When a deaf dog learns a new ability, it feels like a great accomplishment. Conversely, laid back dog owners often love that deaf dogs are more than content to just relax and snuggle with you as you watch tv. There are even deaf dogs that excel at agility training.

The only personality exceptions that may not mesh well with a deafie include people that are easily frazzled or very impatient. When it comes to Natchez, I tend to laugh off situations that others may find frustrating. Unlike a hearing dog, Natchez will sometimes simply refuse to look at me or turn his head. Rarely, though, will he ever see one of my hand signals and ignore me.

Do you need to be an experienced dog owner to properly train and care for a deaf dog? No. There are some advantages for first-time dog owners when caring for a deaf dog. For example, you do not need to re-learn or replace training knowledge to adapt to training a deaf dog. Many first-time dog owners are also invested in 'doing it right,' which results in a great attitude when it comes to training a deaf dog.

That being said, experienced dog owners can also benefit from deaf dogs. Knowing the basics of dog behavior can help when it comes to reading a deaf dog's body language or other dogs that you encounter.

Ultimately, deaf dogs adjust to their owner's personalities and vice versa. All it takes is time and an open heart.

Quality of Life: Is it Humane to Own a Deaf Dog?

Deaf dogs live fulfilling lives. Most do not realize that they are any different than other dogs. Deaf dogs form strong bonds with their owners and their pet siblings. Deafies don't feel self-pity or disabled. They just want to please their owners and do normal dog things.

When considering the quality of life a deaf dog has, it's important to not humanize the dog too much. What do dogs want out of life? This can often be answered simply: they want good health, mental stimulation, a bond with their owner or family, enrichment and purpose, and security based on routine. Working dogs may need more enrichment and purpose, while a Papillon may desire more of a bond with his owner. But when it comes down to it, not being able to hear does not affect a dog's ability to have a fulfilling life.

It is important to adjust to your dog's needs to provide a better quality of life when he can't hear. Minimize your dog's stress by being patient, physically and visually reassuring, and try not to startle him.

When deafness from old age is combined with other issues such as blindness, incontinence, and a lack of mobility, it's best to discuss your dog's quality of life with your vet. Make a list of all the activities your dog loves

Photo Courtesy
of Lara DePietro

and note which he can no longer partake in. Then chat with your vet about chronic pain along with your other observations.

There are many congenitally blind and deaf dogs that also live long, happy lives.

Time, Money, and Commitment

Puppies and dogs require resources. Bigger dogs require more food, higher vet cost, and their supplies like beds and collars often cost more. Puppies often require more time when it comes to housetraining. Deaf dogs require the same amount of time, commitment, money, and patience when it comes to these, just with a twist.

Time: People that choose to adopt deaf dogs assume there is more of a time investment; therefore, they often put more time into learning about their dogs' needs. This book is a great example. If it were available to me, I would have read it cover to cover before adopting Natchez. I truly read every resource available to me before and after bringing Natchez home. Is this an absolute requirement? Not really, but you will likely feel more confident if you devote time to reading about what to expect.

The same is true about the time it takes to socialize your deaf dog. No, it's not required, but it will benefit your dog. This time investment is no more time-consuming than it would be for a hearing dog, though. I find some additional time that my deaf dog requires involves explaining to people that he is deaf and how to interact with him.

Money: The vet bills for a deaf dog do not differ from that of a hearing dog. Adoption fees for deaf dogs are often sponsored or the same as other dogs. When I adopted Natchez, Zappos happened to have sponsored all adoptions for that day.

Many deaf dogs benefit from training equipment such as vibration collars. You can also purchase additional equipment that can help make life easier, like a harness that identifies your dog as deaf or a pheromone collar or diffuser. Choosing equipment strategically can help save money.

Many deaf dog owners gain understanding and confidence by working with trainers and behaviorists. These can range in price. Some shelters will have adopters sign a contract saying that they will provide their adopted dog with professional help rather than give them up for readoption.

Commitment: When adopting a deaf dog, you are required to commit to rethinking dog ownership in some ways. Learning ASL or a mixture of ASL and other signs takes committing to communicating with your dog in a different way. You must also commit to how you will communicate with your other dogs in relation to your deaf dog.

Committing to figuring out what your dog needs over time is also vital to successfully caring for a deaf dog. Many of these things are not apparent at first.

Adopting a Deaf Adult Dog vs. a Puppy

Whenever you decide to add a furry addition to your household, the question arises of whether or not you should adopt a puppy or an adult dog. Both come with challenges.

There are more available adult deaf dogs at shelters. This may be because some families adopt puppies, not knowing they're deaf. Then, after the puppy grows and fails to learn in a traditional manner, or they discover the puppy is deaf, they give it up to the shelter. This results in a lot of deaf dogs that are on the brink of adulthood. On the other hand, breeders will often bring deaf puppies to shelters, too, as soon as they're old enough to be separated from their mothers.

Puppies require potty training and leash training. Deaf puppies also do not learn bite inhibition in the same way their siblings do, so this will require some time, understanding, and training to learn appropriate behavior. Between milk teeth and puppy nips, if you have children, you may want to consider an adult deaf dog.

Many people gain a lot of satisfaction from raising a deaf puppy. Adopting a puppy allows you to experience the joy of watching your dog learn and explore the world from its earliest moments. One of the biggest advantages of adopting a puppy is that you will know its complete health history and general history.

It can be easier to find adult deaf dogs to adopt from shelters. Like all adult dog adoptions, adult deaf dogs in shelters have been through trauma. Depending on a dog's background, this trauma can affect his behavior, confidence, and trust. Because deaf dogs are often misunderstood by their original owners, they can come from situations that may have included abuse.

On the other hand, some deaf dogs have been fostered and trained, which can make some of the initial work and adjustment easier.

Some people find caring for a deaf senior dog fulfilling. Personally, I've found that providing love, comfort, and plenty of treats and snuggles to an elderly dog is extremely rewarding. Adopting a senior dog has a different emotional resonance than adopting a puppy or an adult dog. It also has some unique benefits that can work well for some people's lifestyles. For example, senior dogs require less exercise and are often housebroken. This can be great for someone looking for a lowkey dog.

Unlike puppies, a senior dog won't chew your furniture, and his deafness often allows him to rest more comfortably throughout the day. If you have considered adopting a senior dog that's deaf or hard of hearing, be sure to consider the additional needs some senior dogs have.

Some programs for finding homes for senior dogs will cover veterinary costs. Many of these "forever foster" non-profits require that you live within a select radius from them since you'll likely need to use a vet they have a relationship with.

If the rescue doesn't cover the cost, you should be prepared to cover vet expenses and have your vet examine the dog to give you an idea of his health needs. For example, a semi-deaf and semi-blind Beagle I cared for couldn't climb up and down our stairs and required surgery for breast cancer and infected teeth. Luckily, our community came together to provide for the cost of her surgery, but if they hadn't, it would have been quite expensive.

*Photo Courtesy
of Kelli and Jason Rakozy
@willowandsushi on IG*

One of the easiest ways to decide if an adult dog or puppy is a better fit for you and your household is to interact with deaf dogs and puppies. Not all deaf dogs are the same. So, one dog may be a better fit for your personality than another.

Most people say, "when you know, you know" or "my dog chose me." This was the case with Natchez. When he entered the meet-and-greet playpen, he bee-lined directly over and leaned into me.

Fostering a deaf dog or puppy can give you the opportunity to see how a specific dog will fit into your life without the pressure to permanently commit. Most importantly, trust your heart and your gut. If it doesn't feel right, walk away and think about it.

How to Prepare When You Decide to Adopt

When it comes to bringing home your new best friend, there are some preparations that can make the transition run a lot smoother. From safety concerns to scheduling and supplies, setting your new deaf dog up for success will also set you up for success as a dog owner.

Decide if Now is the Best Time to Adopt

Likely, if you picked up this book, you're a planner. You've considered adoption and adding to your pet family. But maybe you still have questions regarding if now is the best time to bring home a deaf dog. Similar to having kids, many people will tell you there's no perfect time, and if you wait and wait for the perfect moment, you'll miss out. Although there are definitely times in life when a new addition to your home wouldn't be the most ideal situation.

FUN FACT

Gisele Veilleux

The Dog Liberator is a no-kill animal rescue located in Florida. The shelter was founded by Gisele Veilleux in 2009 and focuses on herding dogs. In 2013, Veilleux published a book entitled Deaf Dogs Hear With Their Hearts, which tells the story of a deaf and partially blind Australian shepherd named China who was rescued from a shelter as a puppy. As of 2019, the Dog Liberator shelter had rescued more than two thousand dogs.

Examining your schedule is always a great idea when it comes to adopting a dog. Keep in mind that your new dog will need daily walks, time to train, and playtime.

Deaf dogs thrive with a routine. Your routine does not need to be identical every day, but you should be able to walk and feed your new buddy around the same time most days. This is all to say, if you're expecting a major change in the near future, you may want to hold off on adopting a new dog.

The following are some situations when you may want to consider postponing deaf dog adoption.

You're Expanding Your Human Family

I would suggest waiting to adopt a deaf dog if your family is about to expand. Children require a lot of care, attention, and time. Because deaf dogs have such profound barks, a newly adopted deaf dog may cause a baby to cry. Additionally, the combination of a newborn crying alongside a deaf dog barking sounds like one of the most stressful scenarios I can imagine.

Another consideration when it comes to adding a deaf dog to the mix with a small child is that dogs, in general, tend to be a bit scared of children. This is because children are closer to eye-level with them, and they like to flail their hands, run, and do all those delightful things we love children all the better for.

Overall, most dog adoption coordinators suggest that frail dogs and puppies under five months don't make the best pets for households with children under seven. This is because puppies still have their pointy and sharp milk-teeth, and children under seven are still learning how to pet and handle dogs. When it comes to deaf dogs, the milk teeth guideline matters a bit more. Many deaf puppies don't learn bite inhibition as quickly as other dogs, so their nips can be a bit more painful.

You're Moving in the Near Future

If you're planning an immediate move, you may want to wait until you're settled in your new home to adopt a deaf dog. Deaf dogs tend to rely on knowing their environment well. The adjustment of two new homes in a row and getting acquainted with a new family can be a bit much to handle for a newly adopted deaf dog.

If your move is more than a month or so away, you likely have enough time to help your new dog adjust to his family, and that can help them better cope with the major change.

Imagine Your Current Life with a Deaf Dog

As you go through your day, think about what would be different if you had a deaf dog to take care of. If you already have a dog or dogs, likely your routine will be very similar, with the chance that daily dog tasks will take a bit more time.

People without any dogs should expect a major shift in how their time is used. From bathroom breaks to adding in time for mental and physical stimulation, a new dog can be as time-consuming as a job.

Often the largest time commitment will be the first weeks and months you bring your deaf dog home. Bringing a new pet into the family requires vigilance and attention. Watching your new deaf dog interact with pet siblings and children is especially important. Keeping an eye on your dog for signs he may need to use the bathroom and to keep out of trouble can also become wearisome for new dog parents.

Most care for a deaf dog can be completed in a matter of short time segments. Longer tasks include going to the dog park, the vet, on walks, and training. Shorter tasks do add up, though.

Overall, when you're planning to adopt a deaf dog, you want the chances of success to be favorable. The unfortunate situation of returning a dog to the shelter is traumatic for the dog and the person returning the dog. The decision to adopt should not be spontaneous or an impulse. It's unfair to both the dog and you if it doesn't work out.

If you do not have the time, energy, or means to adopt a dog, you're better off waiting.

Find a Support System

A group of supports can make a world of difference for new deaf dog owners. A support system can help you vent when you're feeling stressed out and offer advice and reassurance. Reaching out to others before you bring your deaf dog home can provide you a resource from the beginning of your journey.

Friends and family members who have dogs can relate to most situations you'll experience with your new dog. It's great to have a go-to couple of people that you can call or text about your dog. They will celebrate with you as you experience successes and milestones. They can give you advice or just listen when you need to vent.

You can find support from other dog owners through dog training classes or the dog park.

Another great place to meet other deaf dog parents is online. There is a subreddit (r/deafdogs) where you can find experienced deaf dog owners who are always willing to chat about your experience. There are also many apps you can use to connect to dog owners in your neighborhood and deaf dog owners in your city. I've had great luck with the Nextdoor and BarkHappy apps.

Make a Plan

Before you pick up your deaf dog, have a plan in place for the upcoming days, weeks, and months.

Your first-day plan should include where your new dog's crate will be, who will wake up to take your dog out in the middle of the night, and who will stay up with your dog if he is scared and crying. Decide on where you will feed your new dog, how and when you'll introduce him or her to your existing pets, and who will walk her.

Sharing responsibility when it comes to cleaning up potential messes can make the first few days a lot easier, as well. Not procrastinating and keeping a clean environment can prevent little messes from becoming large messes and problems.

Bringing an adorable deafie home for the first time can be very exciting. You may want to share this excitement with friends and others, but I suggest waiting until your dog has settled in a bit before having guests over. The extra guests may cause more confusion for your new dog.

Many new deaf dog owners also experience nerves. This is normal. Coming up with a plan on how to deal with your nerves or stress can be a lifesaver. Remember that it's ok to put your pup or dog in the crate, where he is safe, and take a moment to get a little fresh air and recalibrate. Talking to your support system can also help tremendously.

As for planning for the upcoming weeks and months, finding a veterinarian should be the top priority. Ask friends and family for recommendations and read online reviews. After you find a practice you feel comfortable with, make an appointment for an initial checkup to establish care with your vet. Mention that your dog is deaf. Many vets will make accommodations if needed, including letting you wait in your car instead of the waiting room. Diagnosis and care in case of emergency run a lot smoother if your vet has seen your dog while healthy and has your dog's vet records.

Additionally, know where your dog will stay while you're at work or running errands. If you have any trips planned, decide if you'll use a boarding facility or in-home dog sitter. You may want to interview a few dog sitters or dog walkers, so you're familiar with them if you decide to hire one.

Look into trainers and behaviorists and what type of scheduling and prices they offer. If your dog requires grooming, you can also look into deaf-friendly local businesses.

Remember that you cannot plan for everything, but the more you plan for, the more confident and in-control you will likely feel. Preparing is a great way to promote your success and your deaf dog's success as a new family member.

CHAPTER 5
Preparing Your Home for a Deaf Dog

O nce you've decided to adopt a deaf dog, you will want to make sure your home is ready for his arrival. There will always be things that arise after you bring your new fur-bundle home, but there are many things you can prepare beforehand without investing too much money or time.

Preparing your home can aid in a smoother transition and reduce some of the stress of uncertainty. Making some small changes to your home can also keep your new dog safe and reduce the risk of injury. Furthermore, planning ahead can protect your belongings and keep messes to a minimum and within a smaller area.

Within Your Home

It doesn't take a whole lot of time, effort, or energy to prepare your home before bringing your new dog home, but it will lessen the risk of accidents and complications. Starting inside your home ensures that your dog has a safe place to stay. It also minimizes your stress and anxiety when it comes to trial by error.

Deciding on Where to Locate Beds, Crates, Toys, and Dishes

Dogs come with quite a few accessories. Putting them in the right spots can encourage your deaf dog to feel more comfortable and confident in their new home.

You will likely want to place your deafie's crate in a location where he can see you. This helps your new dog feel like part of the family. It can also be reassuring to have you in sight when you begin crate training your new dog. Many deaf dog owners also find it helpful if their dog watches them leave when exiting. This can decrease the likelihood of separation anxiety.

HELPFUL TIP
Indoor Gates

Safety is of utmost concern when preparing your home for a deaf dog. Many deaf dog owners utilize baby gates throughout the home to keep their dogs confined to areas of the house where they are less likely to get into dangerous situations or may be able to escape. Extra-tall dog gates are available to purchase for larger dogs, which may easily jump over a standard baby gate.

Photo Courtesy
of Kelly Bufano

I also highly recommend a crate mat or comfy bed. I always keep a few extra comfort items like soft toys and towels in Natchez's crate. They can come in handy when your dog is bored or wants to dig before lying down.

One option you may want to consider is pheromone spray for your dog's crate. ThunderDog and Adaptil both make sprays that mimic pheromones that help dogs feel at-home. These calming pheromones can help your dog feel more comfortable in their new crate.

Natchez's crate lives in my living room. When I first brought him home, I put it in a spare bedroom—that was a major mistake. He yowled and yowled. He also scratched, cried, and tore a hole through the metal exterior. I then moved him to the living room beside the tv stand. This helped tremendously. He would stare at me while I watched tv. I was able to give him the thumbs-up, smile, and even go over to pet him a bit. He'd soon fall asleep and sleep through the night.

Eventually, I moved his crate beside the sofa, which was more convenient. (Curious about crate training? I will go over how to crate train your deafie in Chapter 7).

As for your dog's beds, you will want to place a few around your house. Not only do these beds provide a comfortable spot for your dog to lie down, reducing sore joints and bald patches, but they also encourage your deafie to be more independent. Without a comfy bed, your dog will likely want to be in constant physical contact with you.

Place beds where your deafie can see you but also rest comfortably. You may find that areas that do not receive direct airflow from overhead vents offer more restful sleep for your deaf dog since deafies can be sensitive to scents carried on air drafts and temperature changes.

Most dog owners place their dogs' food bowls in the kitchen. This works well for deafies, too. The smooth floor surfaces make it easy to clean if your dog dribbles a bit or makes a mess while eating. I also recommend a food mat beneath the bowls to keep from them slipping around and to catch most of the mess.

Be sure to place your dog's bowls out of the way of foot traffic. Startling a deafie while he is eating can cause him to choke. Being calm and relaxed will also encourage slower eating, which benefits a dog's digestion. So, find a spot that is out of the way but allows your deafie to see his or her surroundings.

It's a good idea to keep some extra water bowls around the house to encourage hydration. Sometimes Natchez gets shy about drinking when his brother is also thirsty, so he'll resort to having a sip of water from his bowl in the nearby bathroom. I've also noticed he doesn't like drinking after certain dogs—it may be due to his scent sensitivity—but having extra water bowls gives me peace of mind that he has constant access to fresh water and discourages toilet drinking.

HELPFUL TIP
Put a Bell On It

Putting a bell on your deaf dog's collar can help you keep tabs on him, especially if he accidentally gets loose from your house or yard! Because deaf dogs can't hear auditory commands, it can be difficult to recall them in these situations. A bell is a simple and effective insurance policy to always know where your dog is.

Your deaf dog will also appreciate having toys available. When you first adopt your deafie, you want to provide a variety of toys. Once you learn more about your dog's play style and toy preference, you can get more of his preferred toys. You will likely want a toy bin to store the toys. A basket or box that your dog can reach into to select a toy to play with as he wishes encourages independence and healthy exercise and mental stimulation.

Your dog's toy bin shouldn't be taller than dog-chest-height. This allows your dog to see down into the bin and reach to pick one out. Place the toy bin in an accessible location. Having several toy bins in the rooms where your dog spends the most time is a good idea.

Preparing a Safe Home

Start preparing your home for your deafie's arrival by unplugging or moving electrical cords that your dog could trip on or bite out of curiosity. The most common include lamps, computer cords, tv cords, alarm clock cords.

Secure lamps, free standing fans, and décor that could get bumped into and knocked over or broken. Take extra precautions during the holiday season and secure decorations like Christmas trees.

Relocate your house plants. Some dogs find houseplants irresistible when it comes to nibbling on the leaves, eating dirt, or using the plant as a potty. Relocating them up and out of reach protects your plants and your dog. Some house plants can be poisonous for dogs while others, such as cacti, can prick and injure a curious deafie.

Plants that are dangerous for dogs come in all shapes and sizes. Some are indoor plants, while others may be lurking in your yard. Here are some plants you will want to keep out of reach of your deaf dog:

Sago Palms: These are highly toxic to dogs. Sago palms can cause liver failure and death. Unlike some other plants, every part of the sago palm is toxic, and they are often sweet, which can make them tempting for some dogs.

Cacti: Not only can cacti stick your dog in the nose, eye, or mouth with its sharp spines, but a dog that is unlucky enough to eat cactus plants can also have severe stomach issues.

Aloe: Despite its soothing properties for people, do not use aloe on your dog or let your dog consume aloe or allow juice. Dogs that consume aloe can respond by vomiting, diarrhea, lethargy, tremors, and central nervous system depression, according to the Central California SPCA.

Other, often less tempting, toxic plants include:

- Poinsettia
- Chrysanthemums
- Azalea
- Castor Bean
- Oleander
- Hollies
- Baby's Breath
- Gladiolus
- Daffodils
- Tulips

- Ivy
- Tomato plants
- Amaryllis
- Begonias
- Milkweed

For a complete list of all plant species that are toxic to dogs, check the ASPCA's Animal Poison Control website: asapca.org/pet-care/animal-poison-control

Survey your home and yard from a dog's perspective. Check which cupboards a dog could possibly open. Relocate any food or cleaning chemicals that they may be able to get into. Be sure to close the lid of your toilet and the bathroom door just in case your deafie decides to drink from the commode (this will prevent your dog from drinking any toilet cleaner or lapping up dangerous bacteria or viruses). You may even want to consider using baby-safe locks for cabinets with household cleaners or foods that may cause your deafie harm.

The garbage can be quite tempting for many dogs, especially deafies with a strong sense of smell. Consider keeping wastebins in cabinets and out of paw's reach.

Checking your screens if you open your windows is a good idea. Be sure screens don't push out easily or have any tears that your dog could make worse. When first bringing your dog home, keep un-screened windows closed.

If you want to go above and beyond, you can temporarily remove the knobs from your stove. This prevents them from accidentally turning on the oven or a burner. While this seems silly for tiny breeds, some larger or extremely agile dogs can hop and climb as well as mountain goats.

Storing Treats and Food

You may find your newly adopted dog (especially if he is a rescue) has a voracious hunger. Consider where and how you store his dog food and treats.

For the first year or more after adopting Natchez, he would do anything in his power to get to his kibble or my cat's. Only the strongest, most secure dog food bins could keep him at bay. We use one designed for the Australian Outback, which works well but isn't the most attractive container on the market.

While Natchez has never scaled the counter, many dogs will try to. I suggest placing your dog's treats in an area that is well out of reach of your dog. This may be on the fridge or at the top of a cabinet.

Outside of the Home

If you can afford to fence-in your yard, you will gain an immense amount of peace of mind and provide your deafie with a safe place to play and exercise. If you have a fence, walk the fence line to ensure there are no gaps your dog can squeeze through. This check should include the bottom of the fence, where many dogs can push their way free or flatten themselves out and scurry under.

Safely store any sharp garden tools and gardening chemicals out of reach of your dog. Pick up any rodent traps or poisons you have put out.

If your backyard does not have a shaded area for your dog, create one. Dogs can suffer from heatstroke when they don't have a respite from the sun. A beach umbrella makes a great temporary or longer-term source for shade.

You will also want to have a water dish for the backyard. Place this bowl out of direct sun to help keep the water cool.

Always supervise your dog when he is in the backyard. Again, curious dogs may nibble plants that can be poisonous. Watching your dog also helps

Photo Courtesy
of Joann Sesser

HELPFUL TIP
Wearable Decals

Deaf-dog decals are a great way to keep your dog comfortable and safe in public. Deaf dogs can be easily startled, especially when approached suddenly or from behind. Wearable decals offer a helpful reminder to strangers that your dog is deaf and people need to exercise caution when approaching. Some wearable decals will also state a reminder to strangers to ask before petting, which is especially important for deaf dogs, which may be overstimulated in unfamiliar situations. These decals can be worn on a vest or even clipped to your dog's leash!

troubleshoot if an emergency health problem crops up. For example, if your dog cries out, then holds his paw up, you can check the area for something sharp or narrow it down to a bug bite.

Keeping your grass short will reduce pests like chiggers and ticks that can bother your dog.

As you prepare your home, you will also want to stock up on all the supplies you need to properly care for your dog. It's easier to have these on-hand rather than run out to the store as needed.

Some basic supplies you'll need include:

- Bed and bedding (possibly a crate mat or bed)
- Crate
- Extra towels and rags
- Food
- Harness and/or collar with reflective material
- Leash
- Nail clippers
- Pet stain remover with neutralizing enzymes
- Several bowls for food and water
- Shampoo
- Toys
- Treats
- Leash storage/rack
- Toy storage
- Rags and towels to clean up accidents

Many deaf dogs benefit from the following supplies:

- An American Sign Language handbook
- A deaf dog signifier (like a clicker)
- A doggie puzzle
- An ID tag that identifies the dog as deaf
- A pheromone diffuser
- A vibration collar
- Pheromone spray

Prepare to clean up spills and accidents. It happens, and it's a part of dog ownership. The joy of owning a deaf dog outweighs the time it takes and the hassle of minor messes. Keep your dog in a contained area and slowly let him have more and more freedom as you establish trust and rules. This will help to minimize messes.

CHAPTER 6
Where to Adopt a Deaf Dog

Finding your new best friend can take a little bit of time. You want to make sure you're making the right decision. Meeting deaf dogs at different rescues and shelters can help introduce you to the perfect deaf dog for you and also get you acquainted with the charming differences between hearing dogs and deaf dogs.

So, where can you find an adoptable deaf dog? First, decide how far you're willing to travel to meet a potential dog or how much you're willing to pay to have a dog transported to your home. If you have your heart set on a particular breed, the likelihood of travel and transport fees rise.

Many local shelters have available deaf dogs, but there are also deaf-dog-specific rescues and websites throughout the U.S.

I suggest starting your search at your local shelters if you want to meet and greet dogs and get acquainted with the adoption process in-person. Many shelters have adoption coordinators that can guide you toward dogs that may be a good fit for your home and lifestyle. They can also put you on a waitlist or call you if they receive a deafie looking for a new family.

Using PetFinder to Narrow Your Search and Preview Potential Dogs

You can use PetFinder to browse available dogs and read about their personalities, background, and training. PetFinder allows shelters, rescues, and individuals to post dogs on their database of available dogs. They do not allow breeders to post pets for profit, though.

To search for a deaf dog on PetFinder, put in your zip code and the distance you're willing to travel to a potential candidate. Then, you can filter your results by selecting "Special Needs." This will show dogs that are congenitally deaf or have acquired deafness. From there, you can narrow down by breed, as well. Keep in mind that some shelters do not list their deafies as special needs.

After you spend some time on PetFinder, you will begin to recognize which shelters are closest to you. You can always check their specific websites since some rescues do not put all new dogs onto PetFinder.

Searching for Potential Adoptees on Deaf Dogs Rock

Deaf Dogs Rock is a leader among deaf dog advocacy groups. They are a charitable non-profit that rescues and sponsors deaf dogs. They also provide information to deaf dog parents and others regarding deafies.

The Deaf Dogs Rock website also has a large compilation of deaf dogs looking for loving homes all across the U.S. Simply go to deafdogsrock.com/available-dogs. Then select your geographical region. You can then limit your search to just your state if you choose. This makes it easy to meet your potential adoptee and save a local dog. If you don't fall head-over-paws in love with a local deafie, you can broaden your search. Like PetFinder, Deaf Dogs Rock allows rescues to post available dogs on their website. They do not house dogs or take in dogs.

Deaf Dog and Breed Specific Rescues

Some rescues focus on certain breeds. If these breeds have high rates of congenital deafness, they often take in both deaf and non-deaf dogs of that breed. There are also some rescues that only take in deaf dogs of a specific breed. For example, White Kisses Great Dane Rescue in Lubbock, Texas specializes in deaf Great Danes. One of the easiest ways to find these dogs is to use a search engine and type in: "deaf [breed] adoption."

Some reputable and popular deaf dog shelters in the United States are listed below.

Amazing Aussies (Double-Merle Australian Shepherds in Arizona)
http://www.amazingaussies.org/

Deaf Dog Rescue of America
http://deafdogrescueofamerica.org/

844-Deaf-Dog

Deaf Dogs of Oregon
http://www.deafdogsoforegon.org/

Double J Dog Ranch (Special Needs Dogs in Idaho)
https://www.doublejdogranch.org/

Great Dane Rescue, Inc (Great Dane Rescue in Michigan)
https://www.greatdanerescueinc.com/

Keller's Cause (Deaf Australian Shepherds)
https://www.kellerscause.com/

Pawsavers (Special Needs Dogs in Ohio)
https://www.pawsavers-rescue.com/

Pets with Disabilities
http://www.petswithdisabilities.org/

Pink Heart Rescue (Double-Merle Rescue in Indiana)
https://www.facebook.com/PinkHeartRescue

Speak for the Unspoken (Special Needs Rescue in Ohio)
speakfortheunspoken.com/

Special Needs Animal Rescue and Rehabilitation (SNARR)
https://snarranimalrescue.org/

Photo Courtesy
of Whitney Machnik

Adoption Fees

FUN FACT
Deaf Dogs Rock

Deaf Dogs Rock is a 501(C)(3) public charity based in Virginia that operates on a national scale to promote the well-being of deaf dogs. The Deaf Dogs Rock website features a searchable page of deaf dogs who are seeking adoption across the United States. Hundreds of deaf dogs listed on this site have already found their forever homes. Like many other online pages, these listings are not overseen by a veterinarian, so it's important to exercise caution and due diligence when using this service. More information can be found at www.deaf-dogsrock.com.

Adoption fees can range from under $100 to about $400. While these costs may seem high for "a dog somebody did not want," but adoption fees cover your adopted dog's complete care while at the shelter in addition to the cost of running a shelter. Once you factor in veterinary care, vaccinations, deworming, microchip, food, and the staff to walk a dog, adoption fees don't seem as expensive. Often these fees are split evenly among all pets that enter the shelter, which means your adoption fee goes to a good cause.

Many people wonder why costs vary among shelters. Different rescues have varying costs and take on a wide range of cases. It's important to keep in mind that rescues that take on "difficult to place" dogs anticipate having to care for dogs they take in for longer periods of time. This can lead to slightly higher costs. Some rescues have higher adoption fees for out-of-state adopters since if someone is willing to travel, they're often willing to pay more.

While I would never recommend choosing a dog based on veterinary cost, there are adoption events and days that can have reduced or waived adoption fees. There are also special events where adoption fees are sponsored by businesses. Natchez would have cost me $150 for an in-state adoption, but when I confirmed that I would be his new mom, the adoption coordinator suggested I wait a couple of days to officially adopt him on Black Friday since Zappos was paying all adoption fees. I figured I could use the saving to splurge on some nicer dog gear for my new best friend.

Understanding If a Shelter is Reputable

Not all dog rescues and shelters are created equal. While rescuing a rescue dog from a poorly-run shelter can take a dog away from a bad situation, you want to keep in mind that your adoption fees may go to helping a bad shelter remain open. Additionally, you also need to know what you're getting yourself into. A bad dog rescue may not adequately socialize their dogs, provide them with appropriate medical care, vet or test adoptable dogs for aggression, or worse.

Reputable rescues follow a well-known standard of care. The sad reality is that the federal government doesn't regulate rescues, although some states do. Most good shelters volunteer to provide care based on strict standards such as the Guidelines for Standards of Care in Animal Shelters. Many larger shelters will post this information on their website. If you're unsure, you can also ask.

A good rescue will also keep their facilities and the dog's living quarters clean. Honestly, many dog shelters don't smell amazing, but there should be evidence of cleaning. Dried feces is a bad sign. A slight waste scent beneath the smell of bleach is okay.

The dogs at the shelter should be cared for. They should also be ready for adoption. A bad shelter may try to adopt out a dog that is too thin or not properly socialized. If a dog cowers or runs away from you, he or she is probably not ready to be a part of your family. If a dog shows his teeth when you approach, they likely are not comfortable with people yet. Sometimes dogs are ready for adoption, but they need additional future veterinary care. Most shelters will cover needed procedures like heartworm treatment and spay/neuter.

Dogs should also receive several walks per day and have plenty of space in their kennels. If a shelter doesn't allow you to view the dogs, despite having them on-site, they may be hiding how they kennel their dogs.

Most importantly, keep in mind, you have the right to not adopt a dog or leave a shelter you suspect isn't caring appropriately for their dogs. Sometimes rescues may try to sell you on a dog they've had for "too long," but if the connection is not there, or the dog won't work for your circumstances, it's ok to walk away.

FUN FACT
Why Are Deaf Dogs Often White?

Deaf dogs frequently have white coats because the cells that determine coat color and the cells that make up the ability to hear come from the same stem-cell source. When this stem cell is missing, dogs do not develop the cells that make hearing possible and usually have an absence of pigment in their fur. Of course, white dogs are not always deaf, and likewise, not all deaf dogs are white!

Questions to Ask About a Potential New Dog Before Adopting

Adopting a new dog is a huge commitment. You want to be fully informed before you sign on the dotted line and promise to keep your dog for the rest of its life. The following questions may or may not be deal-breakers for you, but they will help you know what you're getting into.

Finding out as much as you can about a deaf dog's history can tell you a lot about what to expect. When meeting potential dogs, you may want to ask the adoption coordinator or shelter:

- Was this dog a surrender or stray?
- Is there any information you can give us about this dog's background?
- Did this dog enter the shelter with any health concerns other than deafness?
- Is this dog's deafness congenital or acquired?
- Did this dog experience hunger or starvation?
- How well socialized was this dog, and what work have you done to help him/her?
- Does this dog have any dietary restrictions?
- Has this dog expressed any signs of possible abuse?

Behavior Around Kids, Cats, and Other Dogs

Your home life and future home life should also be a factor in which deaf dog will be the best fit for you. Be sure to ask any of these questions that may apply:

- Does this dog get along well with other dogs of all sizes?
- Will this dog enjoy playing with our current dog?
- Does this dog seem to have a high prey drive?
- Has this dog been tested for compatibility with cats?
- Can this dog live in a household with children?
- What is your rescue's policy if this dog doesn't get along well with my current cat/dog/child?

Existing Training or Problem Behaviors

- Is this dog housebroken?
- Does this dog know any tricks?

67

- Has this dog learned any sign language?
- Is this dog leash-trained?
- What is this dog's energy level like?
- Has this dog been tested for food and toy aggression?
- Does this dog present any destructive behaviors?
- Does this dog express separation anxiety?
- Is there anything I should know about this dog that can help me make an informed decision about adopting him?

Talk it over with your family and come to a decision on which of these questions are most important and what your priorities are regarding your new adoptee. There is no such thing as a perfect dog, but it is reasonable to know what kind of work you may need to put into helping a dog overcome challenges. Keep in mind, a dog's love is well worth any amount of work.

Your dog is more important than the shelter he or she came from, but you want to know your dog is ready to be a part of your family.

CHAPTER 7
Training and Communicating with Your Deaf Dog

Communication is the key to success when it comes to relationships. This is no different for your relationship and success as the owner of a deaf dog. The more you work on communication and the better you communicate your expectations with your deaf dog, the easier life will be for both of you.

As I've mentioned before, deaf dogs have a unique dependence on their other senses. Being highly attuned to using their sense of sight can make them more aware of visual stimuli and visual signals. A more adept sense of smell can make the appeal of treats even more intense.

Without the ability to hear, your deaf dog's training is even more vital. Training encourages safety, confidence, and a stronger bond between owner and dog.

You will see there are many approaches to training a deaf dog. You may have to try several before settling on which is best for your deafie. There is also a very good probability that you will want to employ multiple approaches depending on the situation.

FUN FACT
First Pair of Deaf Therapy Dogs in America

Olaf and Skylar, a duo of deaf shelties, are the first pair of deaf therapy dogs to be certified, according to their owner, Robin Kashuba. These gentle pups were certified by Therapy Dog International in December 2015 and work together to bring joy to everyone they meet. Kashuba published a memoir, chronicling her experiences with hearing-impaired and rescue dogs and detailing how these dogs changed her life. The book, entitled Redemption Has 4 Paws, was published in 2017.

As you work with your dog, remember that patience and consistency lead to better results. A professional trainer or behaviorist can also be a great resource when it comes to understanding what works best for your dog and ensuring you're getting the techniques down pat.

Almost all deaf dog owners sign-train their deafies. Most trainers recommend that hearing dogs learn signs that accompany verbal commands. This allows for more seamless communication. My deaf dog knows about 20 signs. Some are what I refer to as "power commands," while others are typical dog tricks like "shake" or "spin in a circle."

My hearing dog responds to hand signals as well. During training sessions, both dogs learn and watch one another. This helps reinforce the meaning of the hand signals for both dogs. I even challenge them by providing the treat to whichever dog performs the behavior correctly first. Natchez often wins.

Learning commands and how to communicate is essential for your deaf dog's confidence and fitting into your home. How else will your deafie learn the rules and feel proud?

When I first adopted Natchez, he was wild. He didn't know what he should be doing and not doing. He leaped up on side tables, jumped on strangers, and would gobble up any food I happened to set down. Additionally, he accidentally stumbled into the cat, resulting in a few scratches to his nose.

After learning the ASL sign "sit," followed by several other signs, Natchez's behavior significantly improved. It was as if the lack of order and communication before starting sign training left him aimlessly naughty. Learning that there are rules and a system of communicating those rules made him feel more confident in himself and his understanding of his role and the rules that accompany that role. Teaching him the "point" command to direct his line of vision to where the cat was hiding also prevented plenty of needless scratches.

Deafies, like other dogs, need structure. Hand signals are an essential part of this structure. Once your dog learns the basics, you can build from there.

ASL or Dog Training Hand Signals

One of the first things you must decide when training a deafie is if you will use common dog training signals or American Sign Language (ASL). Which is best for your dog?

Most deafies benefit from ASL since there are more signs to use. Because ASL is an established system of communication, those who know ASL can communicate with your deafie without needing to learn a new language.

One drawback of ASL is that the signs are often smaller and can have more subtle differences between them. For obvious reasons, your deafie's "come here" sign needs to be large enough and obvious enough that your dog can see it from a distance. Another is that signs that require both hands can make it difficult to hold a treat. Many dog owners (whether their dog can hear or not) run into this issue while holding a leash.

If you have a hearing dog that has been previously trained with common dog training hand signals, you may be better off sticking to those since your hearing dog may become quite confused when commands suddenly have two different signals. Of course, some deafies learn commands while at the shelter or before being adopted out from a litter. These dogs are frequently taught typical dog training hand signs.

I usually recommend a hybrid of mostly ASL with some modifications that will work better from a distance or for dogs that cannot see well. Most ASL signals are intuitive to learn.

For Natchez, the ASL signs are often easier for him to comprehend since many typical dog training hand signs can seem to blend together when the verbal accompaniment cannot be heard. For example, the typical dog command for sit is to hold a treat between your thumb and forefingers, with the back of your hand facing your dog. Many people then say "sit" while moving this hand over their dog's head, encouraging the dog to drop his butt. But through the eyes of a deaf dog, this hand movement seems non-specific. Furthermore, as the hand moves closer to the dog's head, he often wants to back up to maintain sight of your hand since that is how he "hears" you.

It's also important to keep in mind that sign-trained deafies look to your hands for messages. If you speak like a mob boss, you may find your dog frustrated and confused that you keep making the "sit" sign without acknowledging his behavior or rewarding him. Seeing as the ASL sign for sit is so unique, I do not accidentally repeat "sit" during conversations with friends and family.

Most importantly, you want your method of training to reflect your dog's needs and what works best for you both.

Deaf Dogs and Your Body Language

Deafies often watch their owners closely. Between your body language, facial expressions, and actions, you will communicate a wide array of messages to your deaf dog. This can lead to him having the uncanny ability to predict what you're going to do or say.

As you sign train your deafie, keep in mind that he's mostly watching your hands while also watching your mouth, face, and posture. As you sign commands, you will likely want to say the command, as well. Additionally, you want to celebrate your dog's success through your facial expressions, posture, and with a "good dog" sign.

When your deafie is misbehaving, you want to show your disapproval with your body language and facial expressions. When Natchez starts to get into trouble, I often stand with my hands on my hips, shake my head "no," and frown. If his action is more immediate, I flick my finger in a "no-no" gesture.

71

For deaf dogs that are fearful or reactive, your body becomes a tool to tell them you have everything under control and that they're safe. When Natchez and I go on a walk, I stand between him and other dogs or people. This tells him that he's protected.

Soon, you'll find that your communication with your deaf dog comes naturally. Like all dogs, you learn to read one another. You will notice soon after beginning to teach your deaf dog to read sign language that he or she will watch your hands, waiting for a command.

Training a Deaf Dog

To begin training your deaf dog, you must first have a grasp of your dog's motivation and learning style. If your deafie is highly food motivated, congratulations, your training sessions will go a lot smoother. For dogs that are not highly food motivated, you will want to invest in some higher value treats or find out if your dog has another reward that can work.

When it comes to high-value treats, try to choose treats with a potent scent. Training treats with fish in them often work well. Peanut butter on a spoon can also snap an unmotivated dog to full attention. I recommend only using these rewards during training to increase their value.

Dogs that don't seem interested in treats can sometimes be encouraged by a high-value toy, instead. When using a toy

FUN FACT
Cole the Deaf Dog

An adorable deaf pit bull in New Jersey, named Cole, spreads love and hope in his community as a local therapy dog. Cole's owner, Chris, an elementary school music teacher, has brought Cole to his school in order to help his students develop compassion for people and animals with disabilities. Chris and Cole have even spread their message of inclusion and compassion on the Rachel Ray show, GMA, Entertainment Tonight, and Access Hollywood! Cole now has a YouTube channel where he "reads" bedtime stories, as well as an Instagram account (@colethedeafdog) where his four thousand followers can keep up with Cole's numerous community appearances.

as a reward, you give the dog the toy when the command is performed correctly. Let him enjoy the toy for about 15 seconds before retrieving.

Reward your dog for successful training sessions, too. After sitting and following commands, your dog will appreciate a walk or some leash-free time in the backyard. Over time, this will help your deafie want to partake in training.

Beginning a Successful Training Routine

Training a deaf dog is not more difficult than training a hearing dog. The only difference is your mode of communication and the need to keep in mind your dog's unique needs.

I've worked with Natchez for over five years. I still enjoy training him, and he still loves training sessions. We have worked with various behaviorists and trainers on our journey. Along the way, I've made plenty of mistakes, especially when I began training Natchez. If you're worried about not having the skills to train a deaf dog, don't worry—all you need is time and commitment. As our current trainer likes to say, "Don't worry. You can't really break them."

In this section, I've included what has worked best for my dog, what other deafie owners have found useful, and what I've learned from several veterinarians and trainers. Not all deaf dogs are the same, but this advice should work well for many.

One question that often comes up is, "Should I use positive or negative reinforcement?" to train my deafie. In this book, positive reinforcement refers to rewarding the dog when the desired behavior is performed. Negative reinforcement is when you discipline your dog when an undesirable behavior is performed. Discipline does not mean to inflict physical force or punishment. In the case of your deafie, discipline means to give them a sign for "no" and intervening to stop the undesired behavior.

To answer this question, I would first recommend never spanking your deaf dog. Because deaf dogs are so touch-sensitive and easy to startle, this can have a disastrous effect on your dog's trust and nerves. It can also lead to confusion once you begin tapping your deaf dog to get their attention.

I also do not think a 100% positive reinforcement training routine is possible. You will want to use 100% positive reinforcement for commands, but when your dog is misbehaving, chewing up a book, or jumping up on the counter, positive reinforcement does not come into play. Removing the book or removing your dog from the kitchen is technically negative reinforcement. If you are going to counter-condition your deafie from barking, you may want to use collar tugs or a prong under the guidance of a qualified trainer.

This means you will rely on positive, treat-based (or reward-based) techniques for teaching your dog what you want and behaviors they should be doing. When your dog misbehaves, you will want to stop the bad behavior and redirect them to a positive behavior.

Training sessions should be relatively distraction-free, especially when you first begin training your dog. For deaf dogs, you can achieve this by choosing a room in your home that doesn't get a lot of foot traffic. Close the curtains or blinds and shut off the television. If you have a ceiling fan, you may want to switch it off as well, just in case.

Choose a room where your dog has space to move around. Include a bowl of water in the room. Treats can make your dog quite thirsty.

I strongly suggest starting with a fanny pack-like bag with treats in it. This will free up your hands. I use a bag that clips around my hips. Over time, this bag can signal to your dog that it's time to learn. When I put my bag on, Natchez knows it's time to begin. He practically worships this bag and is always extremely attentive and on his best behavior when it comes out.

I find it easier to signal with my dominant hand and reward with the other. This prevents your dog from lunging at your signing hand when you teach him commands like "shake" or "down." It also makes him very aware that he needs to wait for the "correct" signal before he can have his reward. This is a must when your deafie learns to perform multiple commands in a row.

You want your deafie to know that you are offering rewards for training. Let your deafie smell a treat in your hand and allow him to take one or two from you. Do the same if you're using an alternative reward like a toy.

If you have a multi-dog family, teach each dog new tricks and behaviors individually and separately. This allows them to devote their full attention to you. After a session or two, you can have them perform the behavior together. If one dog already knows the behavior and performs it consistently, you can bring him in to set the example for your deafie that is learning the command.

Some training can be quite rigorous. Learning to sit, then lie down, then get back up can feel like doing push-ups to your dog. Keep this in mind, and don't overwork him in the first session where he's learning very physical commands like these.

Allow your dog to take breaks during training. If you notice your dog becoming increasingly more impatient or having a harder time paying attention, take a break. Look for signs of stress or frustration. Natchez will whine if he's feeling overwhelmed or frustrated. I do not push him too hard during these times. We take a break and get back to it later. You can also revert back to a command your dog has down really well to help him feel better.

Training sessions work well in stints of about ten to fifteen minutes. Puppies may need shorter sessions than that, though.

While your dog is learning a new behavior or command, schedule training sessions daily or every other day. Train with your dog at least a few times per week after that to maintain the behavior and begin to pepper in the new command in your everyday interactions with your dog.

When it comes to your first few training sessions, start small and go slow. It can be helpful to have an extra person in the room to assist.

Keep in mind that all dogs have different gifts and capabilities. Maintain realistic goals and expectations, but don't be afraid to challenge your dog. You may be surprised by how talented, smart, and capable he is. Keeping a journal or a video record of your dog's training can help you see just how far he has come. Posting pictures of your dog's successes on social media can be a fun way to celebrate your dog and bring positive attention to talented deafies.

The most important thing when it comes to training your dog is to stay positive and celebrate your dog's accomplishments. Enter your training time in a happy and supportive frame of mind and choose a time that you don't feel pressured to hurry through the session. If you're in a bad mood (maybe your deafie got into the trash), it's ok to skip a session. Just be sure you don't completely fall off-track. Training should be fun for you and your dog. A dog that enjoys training will want to learn more.

Photo Courtesy
of Julia Philp

Using Hand Signals

Keep Hand Signals Distinct and Obvious

Before you begin training your dog, decide on which hand signals you want to use. Practice before introducing them to your dog through training. Watch videos through websites or apps that show the ASL version of the sign (I've included some resources at the end of this section) and the typical dog training command.

When you first begin using a hand signal, exaggerate it to make it clearer to your dog. Hold your hands out from your body. If a signal is too complex or too similar to an existing hand signal that you use, modify it or go another route.

One trainer suggested that I include my foot for a "leave it" signal. She wanted me to tap next to the dropped treat to signal for Natchez to ignore the treat. This failed miserably. Not only was he terrified, but I felt like I was performing a dance—I am uncoordinated and a terrible dancer. Needless to say, Natchez does not know the traditional "leave it" command. Instead, he follows the "no-no" finger gesture, which has the same outcome.

You may want to consider wearing white gloves during your training sessions to make your hands more visible.

"Good Dog" vs. "Correct" Clicker Signal

Dogs learn through training and during passive times. Some deafies also tend to be a bit nervous or need reassurance that what they're doing is ok. Additionally, you don't want to have to give your dog treats in order for him to do what he's supposed to. Because of these reasons, you will want to teach your dog two separate signs: "good dog" and "correct."

For "good dog," keep your sign simple. I use the thumbs-up. This tells Natchez that everything is ok and that I'm proud of him. I use this when he's behaving but not being told to perform a command. This can be used if your dog is relaxed around strangers, not jumping up, or lying beside the sofa instead of on it. You should accompany "good dog" with a sporadic treat when you first teach this sign. This connects the sign to a reward. Over time, you can give fewer treats as it becomes more of a psychological reward to your dog.

Good Dog

Many trainers recommend using a clicker, verbal praise, and treats when training a hearing dog. Obviously, deaf dogs cannot hear clickers. In order to provide the same instantaneous effect that

Yay or celebration

your dog did the command correctly, you need a sign. A fast and dramatic sign does the trick. I hold my hand in a loose fist with my thumb pointed upward and flick my wrist to the side. This quick flick tells Natchez he did the command correctly and will receive a treat as his reward.

Unlike "good dog," "correct" should always be followed by a treat. It is a promise or contract you're making with your dog that he or she can rely on. You can give the "good dog" sign for a job well done without a treat, though.

Other celebratory signs can tell your dog he or she is doing well. "Happy hands," or "yay" in ASL, can tell your dog that you're very pleased with his performance.

Useful Commands and Where to Start

After your dog learns that you have treats, he will want to know how he can earn some. He may stare at you, paw your treat hand, or even cry a little while waiting for one. These are all clear signs that your dog is ready to learn.

"Sit"

"Sit" is a great foundational command. When paired with "stay," it becomes a very effective tool.

The ASL sign for "sit" looks like two legs (your index and middle finger) sitting on a bench (the index and middle fingers of your other hand). This can be performed by extending your right index and middle fingers and touching the center knuckles of your left index and middle finger.

To teach your deafie to sit, show your dog the "sit" sign. You can get his bottom to lower by raising your hands, encouraging him to lift his head and

Sit

drop his butt, or by gently pushing his bottom to the floor. As soon as your dog sits, flick your "correct" sign, and give him the treat. Repeat this a few more times. You should be able to stop pressing on his bottom or raising your hands. This command takes most dogs five to ten minutes to learn.

Reinforce this command over the course of a few weeks to fully instill it.

"Shake Hands" or "Give Me Paw"

Teaching your dog to shake can be very useful for nail clipping, if your dog gets a burr, or in similar circumstances. This is a great skill to link to sit.

To teach your deafie to "shake hands," have him sit. Then move your hand and gently wrap it around your dog's paw. If your dog naturally lifts his paw, great! If not, that's ok, too. Give him the "correct" sign, then his treat.

Shake Hands

Repeat this several times, gradually lifting your dog's paw off the floor. After a few minutes, you should be able to put your hand out, flat toward your dog, and he should lift his paw onto your hand. When this happens, immediately flash your "correct" sign and provide the treat.

"Stay"

Stay is a great way to control your deafie when new people come over or to keep your dog safe.

Link "stay" to "sit." Once your dog is sitting, lift your hand upward, palm facing your dog (like you would gesture 'stop'). Wait a few seconds. If your dog

Stay

does not move, sign "correct" and give him a treat. If your dog moves, start over.

Over time, you should be able to walk away or extend your dog's stay time by holding your palm toward your dog. Release him using the "correct" sign.

Point Training

Point training your deaf dog is one of the most versatile and useful skills you can have. This multi-purpose command can alert your deafie to look in a direction or to get him to go where you want. I use it to tell Natchez where to go and wait. It also comes in handy when the cat is nearby, and he doesn't know she's there.

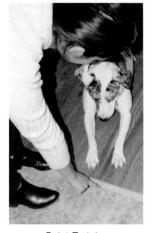

Point Training

To teach your dog to respond to your pointing, hide a few treats through-out the room while your dog is away. When your dog comes in the room, point your finger where each treat is hidden. This connects the idea of direct-ing your dog's attention to a reward and, over time, to where you want him to look or go.

This skill can take several sessions and several weeks to perfect, but it is well worth your time.

"Touch the Hand"

Touch the Hand

"Touch the hand" is a great com-mand to keep your dog's attention and for your dog to ask for your attention. When successfully learned, your dog will poke you with his nose to get your attention. Natchez leaps into the air to touch my hand, which I can use to get him to jump onto agility equipment.

To teach this command, simply hold your hand flat and gently touch your dog's nose. Then give the "correct" sign and a treat. Repeat this. After a few minutes, pull your hand away from your dog and increase the distance between your dog's nose and your hand.

Where to Learn ASL

If you are interested in learning ASL, there are many resources available to you. For looking up specific words, handspeak.com or signingsavvy.com have easy to use search functions and clear videos demonstrating the signs.

To learn more ASL, I recommend looking for a local class. These are often offered at local community colleges, schools, and libraries. You can also learn ASL from online classes and videos or through an app. The app Sign Language ASL- Pocket Sign is user-friendly and fun. ASL Dictionary is a great app to have available for reference, as well.

ASL Connect through Gallaudet University offers free online lessons with great videos.

ASL Rochelle's Youtube channel is very helpful for learning a broad array of ASL phrases and words. Christina Lee from Deaf Dogs Rock's YouTube channel has some excellent lessons on teaching dogs sign language.

INTERMEDIATE COMMANDS
With Eric Melvin

Photo Courtesy of Eric Melvin

Eric and Angelyne

I'm the owner and trainer of Angelyne and Maddie "the Amazing" DEAF Cattle Dogs. I also help train and inspire other deaf dogs and their humans to create a loving and meaningful life together. I created a series of cues and hand signs from a need for basic training as well to build a foundation for the advanced vocabulary we use for bonding, educating, and entertaining.

I didn't teach Angelyne or Maddie with American Sign Language (ASL). I created a "unique to us" training program that includes hand signs, touch, vibration, lights, facial expression, body language, energy changes and smell. Rather than hand signals I think in terms of cues and vocabulary. Our cues and signs are simple and can be expanded on. At the height of Angelyne's career and abilities, she had a vocabulary of 63 different cues. Our array of cues and vocabulary is large but each is simple and effective. Our cues and vocabulary work for us, how we live, communicate and thrive together in all areas of our life.

In your own journey with your deaf dog, you may find that simpler is better when teaching hand signals and commands. With that said, here are some useful basic and intermediate hand signals you can teach to help you more effectively communicate with your dog.

Focus:

Flat, open hand to closed hand like a fist. All our commands begin from the "focus" position

Come (up close):

Opposite of focus. Open hand, palm up to closed hand like a fist.

Lay:

Two fingers slapped or pointed towards the ground

Drop it:

Start with focus (closed fist) bend wrist down then back up again

Get the ball:

Open hand shaped like actually hold- ing a ball, bend wrist up and down

Rise / stand from laying position:

Focus (closed fist), open, cupped hand, palm up, lift hand

Eric Melvin's Tips For Living With And Training Your Deaf Dog

■ Deaf dogs cannot hear hazardous things such as cars, weather, con- struction and wildlife. Please follow the leash law policies for the areas you live, work and play and travel. Build a sense of trust with your dog so she looks back at you frequently when given time off-leash. I use a 10 second rule with Angelyne and Maddie. When off leash if they don't look back at me in 10 seconds I go to them and leash them.

■ Deaf dogs can communicate with more than just hand signs including body language, facial expressions, touch, lights and vibrations. The essen- tials are come, sit, stay, come, down, wait, lay, good, no and watch / focus.

■ Find what motivates your dog. When you find those things use them as positive training tools!

■ Be consistent in your communication and practice, practice, practice!

■ Buy a tag for your dog's collar that reads: I AM DEAF, the dogs name, your name and phone number

■ Place a bell on your dog's collar so you can hear and find her easily if she's out of sight

- Use flashlights, treats, fans, laser pointers and vibrations to get your dogs attention. Be careful of OCD behaviors developing with lights and lasers. Use them as positive training tools.

- Let your dog know when you are leaving the room or house so not to startle and confuse.

- Wake a deaf dog gently. Use a piece of food at first to make it a positive experience. You can also blow softly to wake them. Be sure that you are the first thing your dog sees / smells when they open their eyes. I pet Angelyne and Maddie on the side of their heads softly with one hand while I give them a "thumbs up" with the other hand as they open their eyes. Some deaf dogs may bite, startle, or jump when you wake them. That can be avoided with proper positive training.

- Arrange furniture around the perimeter of room with the center open so your deaf dog can see everything in the room at all times so not to startle or surprise when your or a guest enters the room.

- Keep all cleaning / automotive chemicals, medicines, food or other items up high, or in areas / cabinets / closets that the dog cannot get to. Many

Angelyne the Amazing Deaf Cattle Dog

deaf dogs can smell stronger than hearing dogs and sometimes search out those items out of curiosity, hunger or boredom.

- Leave a light on in your house when you leave and your deaf dog is there alone. Deaf dogs are sensitive to light. When they see changes in light, shadows and darkness they may become startled. Light is good for deaf dogs because it can help build their confidence and comfort level.

- Don't leave toys or food out when you leave. You won't be able to supervise them and protect them from chewing / playing and possibly choking.

- In new and familiar places shut doors to rooms you don't want your dog going to. Deaf dogs wander based on smell and curiosity. If deaf dogs don't see us they get anxious. Keep your dog close and don't allow them to wander into areas where you can't see them. When in doubt use the leash!

- Once you have developed a bond with your dog and she knows the way around the house play hide and seek with him / her. I trained Angelyne and Maddie to be able to find me based on my scent when I leave a room. Most of the time I let them know when I'm leaving a room but other times I don't so I can test their ability to trace my scent. Once they find me I give a treat in the beginning until she knew she was doing a good thing to come and find me. Now when I'm not in their sight they come look for me every time!

You can learn more about Eric Melvin and his work with Angelyne and Maddie on their website: www.ericandangelyne.com

Follow them on Facebook: "Eric and Angelyne the Amazing DEAF Cattle Dog"

Motivating a Deaf Dog

When it comes to motivating your deafie to learn, you want to keep the reward worth the work.

Keep training fresh and exciting with high-value treats. You may want to switch the type of treats to keep things fresh or surprise your dog with a new toy at the end of a really strenuous session.

Always celebrate, smile, and have fun. Don't worry about laughing if your deafie does something goofy.

Some deaf dogs inherently want to learn and please you. This is especially prevalent with many double-merle breeds since most come from herding and working backgrounds. Many deafies are just so thrilled to have someone that can communicate with them that they're willing to do almost anything you ask.

Keeping a Deaf Dog's Attention

One thing you will learn quite quickly is that gaining a deaf dog's attention can be challenging. Luckily, keeping that attention is a lot simpler.

To get your deaf dog's attention, you can use a vibration collar. Other methods include waving at your deafie. If your dog is lying, standing, or sleeping nearby, gently tap your dog's shoulder. When your dog looks at you, be sure to give the "good dog" signal.

You can teach your deafie to continue to watch you using treats and some patience. You can do this by allowing your deafie to smell the treat, then tapping next to your eyes. The movement of your finger tap should gain his attention. When he looks at your finger, flash the "correct" sign. Repeat this several times until your dog has it down pat. Then you can hold your finger for longer and longer periods of time, only giving the treat if he maintains attention. Note that your dog does not have to make direct eye contact since that can be intimidating for some dogs. If your dog breaks his attention, restart.

Crate Training

Successful crate training can do wonders for your peace of mind and your deafie. When a dog is crate trained, he learns to recognize his crate as his own safe room or den. All of my dogs love their crates and voluntarily go inside them.

Knowing that your dog is safe and secure in a crate while you're out of the house is valuable. When your dog is secured in a crate, he won't be able to tear through the trash or accidentally get injured. Crate training can also protect your possessions. A dog who's in a crate can't pee or poo on your carpet or tear up your sofa.

When you travel, bring along your dog's crate, so he can have his safe spot to relax. You can also go out and explore without worrying about what your dog is doing in the hotel room, guest suite, or other accommodation. Crate training your dog also prepares him for boarding.

To crate train your deafie, choose a crate that provides good ventilation and enough room for your dog to turn in a full circle. Place the crate in an area where you spend time. Orient the crate so your deaf dog can see you.

Many dog owners make the mistake of placing the crate in a room that nobody goes in. This isolates your dog and makes him feel like he's being punished. Deafies, like other dogs, are social and want to be with the family. Yes, your dog will likely bark, whine, cry, and throw a temper tantrum for a week or two when he finally has to stay in his crate with the door closed. That's normal. As long as he's not hurting himself, your dog will settle down. Be reassuring with that thumbs up, stay in the room, and even pet your dog through the crate.

To begin crate training your deafie, set up the crate with a comfy crate bed or mat and a few comfort items. Toss a few treats into the crate and let your dog go in of his own volition. If your dog refuses to go in, you will want to entice your dog with even higher value treats or toys. Try peanut butter or a fish-based treat—these usually have the strongest scent. Do not force your dog into the crate since this will create a negative association with the crate. Remember to give your dog time and be patient.

Repeat this over the course of a few days. Soon, your dog will enter the crate without hesitating, close the door behind him and give him a few more treats. Let him out and love on him.

Do this several more times over the course of a few days, increasing the amount of time the door stays closed. Once you're up to a few minutes, close the door and sit nearby. Remember to give the thumbs-up and smile at your dog. Let him stay in the crate for ten minutes or so. Then let him out. Double the time and relax and watch tv or read nearby, so your deafie feels more comfortable. After a while, your deafie should fall asleep or relax. At this point, he is fine to be left in the crate overnight or while you're out of the house.

Vibration Collars

Vibration collars work well for many deaf dogs. I personally had limited success with Natchez, but many deaf dog owners swear by them for recall.

This means when a dog is running loose in the yard, the vibration should prompt the deafie to return to his owner.

You can train your deafie to do this by securing the collar tightly enough around your dog's neck so that he can feel the vibration through his fur. Then press the button, flash the "correct" signal, and provide a treat. After a while, your dog should begin to look to you for a treat when he feels the vibration.

After your dog connects the vibration to looking at you and receiving a treat, you can then graduate to teaching your deafie how to be recalled. To do this, put your deafie on the leash and go into the backyard. Keep your dog at heel position. Then give him slack. As he begins to walk away, press the vibration button. When he turns to you, give him the "correct" signal and a treat. You can increase the distance over time by adding a rope to his leash. Once he has the behavior down, you can try off-leash recall in a fenced-in area. Eventually, you can discontinue treats.

Learning to Walk Nicely On-Leash

Leash etiquette can be quite different for different dogs. Starting with the mildest intervention, then progressing from there, if needed, is a good course of action.

Begin leash etiquette training by walking with your dog. If your dog

Photo Courtesy of Janet Santilli

begins to pull, stop walking, and wait for your dog to turn to you. Then, command your deafie to touch the hand. Flash the "correct" sign, provide a treat, and keep walking. If your dog pulls, again, repeat. This teaches your dog that he's not going to make progress unless he walks with a loose leash.

The next step if the first tactic doesn't work is to use a front-clipping harness. This redirects your dog to the side when he pulls, discouraging pulling over time.

If your dog continues to pull, it can become a safety issue. Pulling can strain your arm and body and can undermine a secure hold on your dog. You can consider using a prong collar. I do not recommend a choke collar or Thunder harness. Choke collars can cause permanent damage to your dog's throat. I found the Thunder harness to be ineffective. A prong collar applies even pressure all the way around your dog's neck. It gradually becomes tighter, so your dog will slow down when it becomes uncomfortable. I suggest you consult a trainer or behaviorist should you reach this step, though.

Managing Problem Behaviors

All dogs are unique. Some of their quirks can be rather disruptive, annoying, and upsetting. Learning to help your deafie manage these behaviors can improve your life, your relationship with your dog, and your dog's life.

Barking

Barking is one of the most difficult behaviors to break for a deaf dog, mostly because he cannot hear himself. Natchez was a reactive barker. He barked at strangers and other dogs on walks. He would get overly excited and bark at house guests sometimes. I recommend getting to the bottom of why your dog is barking and then working from there.

One common mistake people make is accidentally positively reinforcing barking. This often happens when a guest comes over. The dog barks at the guest, then to try to get the dog to stop barking, the guest is encouraged to give the dog treats. This tells the dog that his behavior is appropriate. Instead, treat your dog during moments he is silent. If you can flash the "correct" signal, that is even better.

Another strategy that works for some people is to put a leash on their dog and give it a slight tug when he barks, providing a slight negative reinforcement.

Because barking is a difficult challenge to overcome with a deafie, it can be a great reason to contact a trainer.

Playing Rough

Dogs learn how to moderate their playful bites, nips, and energy by playing with littermates. When a hearing dog nips another puppy, the other puppy will shriek or yelp and stop engaging in play. Through this negative association, a hearing dog learns boundaries and limitations. Sometimes, deafies do not learn this connection. This can lead to rough play habits.

If your deafie plays too rough with you, biting, scratching, tugging on your hands, immediately stop playing and walk away. If this doesn't remedy the problem, try having a second person squirt your deafie with a water bottle when he gets a little too rough.

Until you feel confident that your deafie can play gently, do not let him play unsupervised with other dogs or kids. This is a "just in case" precaution. Sometimes other dogs don't know how to react to deafies and can become retaliatorily aggressive and injure or provoke your deafie.

Unwanted Chewing

Some deafies can be a bit orally fixated. Chewing can also be a sign of stress or anxiety (often separation anxiety). Chewing can become a health concern if your deafie swallows something dangerous.

If your deafie excessively chews, consult your veterinarian. Be very vigilant about what is within reach of your deafie. Crate training your dog is the best way to protect your possessions while your dog is alone.

It's also important to provide your dog with appropriate chewing opportunities with a variety of toys. If chewing continues, consult a trainer or behaviorist.

When a Behaviorist or Trainer Is Best

Training a deaf dog can be difficult. Some dogs just need more than the owner can offer. Some owners do not have the time or know-how to effectively train their dogs. If you feel overwhelmed or confused, don't feel bad! It's important to seek the help of an expert when you hit a roadblock.

Dog training professionals can give you insight into your dog's motivations, needs, and provide you with techniques that will work best for your dog.

Choosing a Behaviorist or Trainer

Dog trainers and behaviorists can be an expensive investment. That makes choosing the right one even more important. Every dog owner wants to invest their time, money, and dog's energy into a trainer that will work for them. This is why I suggest you take your time selecting a qualified and helpful trainer.

Many dog owners are not sure if they need a behaviorist or a trainer. Some trainers call themselves behaviorists, but if they do not possess a master's degree or higher in applied animal behavior, they are not technically a behaviorist. Certified Applied Animal Behaviorists have Doctorates in Veterinary Medicine with a residency in animal behavior afterward.

You will want to use a Certified Applied Animal Behaviorist if your regular vet suggests it will help or if your deafie experiences severe anxiety or has an extreme behavioral condition. These veterinarians can prescribe medications and guide you through why your dog expresses a certain behavior. They can also diagnose any underlying physical issues that may cause your dog's problems. For example, compromised eyesight can lead to heightened nervousness. An animal behaviorist will give very clear guidance and instructions as to how you can best help and train your dog in relation to his issues.

Many dogs do not need a veterinary behaviorist but most greatly benefit from working with a trainer.

When contacting a behaviorist or trainer, ask questions and check for their credentials. Some common certifications include

- Certification Council for Professional Dog Trainers
- International Association of Animal Behavior Consultants
- Association of Animal Behavior Professionals
- Certified Behavior Adjustment Training
- International Association of Canine Professionals
- National Association of Dog Obedience Instructors

You can always ask for references, as well. Most good trainers will offer to meet you and your dog to discuss a plan, and so you can see how they interact with your dog.

Always ask about their experience working with deaf dogs. They should be able to tell you how they adjust their techniques for deaf dogs. I would suggest asking if a deafie owner would volunteer to be a reference for them.

Ask how they would describe their training style, why they enjoy training dogs, and what kind of results they guarantee. You may also want to ask about their approach to positive or negative reinforcement and discuss your dog's specific needs. I find trainers that will come to your home often see a truer glimpse of your dog's behaviors.

Some trainers ask for a flat fee and will work with you and your dog until your dog's behaviors are handled. Others charge by the session. I have had the best luck with a trainer that charged a large flat fee upfront and worked with me until I was satisfied. She also is happy to return for intermittent help if needed. Because she charges a flat rate with a contract, she does not charge for additional "tune-up" sessions.

Most importantly, you want to feel like your trainer is meeting your needs and expectations and can communicate effectively with you. You are ultimately the one who has to do the work, but clear instruction and adequate support make a world of difference.

CHAPTER 8
Socializing with Other Dogs

Dogs are naturally social animals. They are born into litters and form packs. As they interact with one another, they communicate through body language, verbal cues, and actions. Many of these cues are subtle yet complex. This can create a disadvantage for deaf dogs since they do not pick up on verbal cues from their canine counterparts. Most dogs learn appropriate social skills from puppyhood, beginning just a few days after they are born. These skills are further built upon as a puppy's senses begin to fully form and adapt to the world around it. [1] During this time, dogs learn how to play and interpret one another's cues. Because deafies cannot hear, they miss out on a major chunk of their littermates' and their mother's social cues. This can result in a deafie who's socially awkward.

Because some deaf dogs are at a disadvantage, it's important to help them learn and build their skills in a safe and supervised environment.

*Photo Courtesy
of Mary Thompson*

1   Tiffany J. Howell, Tammy King and Pauleen C. Bennett, "Puppy Parties and Beyond: The Role of Early Age Socialization Practices on Adult Dog Behavior," Veterinary Medicine 2015, no. 6 (2015): 143-153, https://www.ncbi.nlm.nih.gov/pmc/articles/PMC6067676/.

Photo Courtesy of Tracey Gant

Set Your Dog up for Success

When you choose to bring a deaf dog into your home, you want him to experience the best possible life. Of course, some dogs just aren't what many people call "dog-dogs," which is to say, they just don't express much interest in other dogs. This can often be the case with deaf dogs since some have experienced trauma from their inability to read other dogs' cues. Some may prefer the company of people to other dogs because they feel fearful, and their human acts as a security blanket.

When introducing two dogs, it's best to do so in neutral territory in a fenced area where they can meet off-leash (leashes can cause tension since they can make dogs feel both trapped and defensive of their owners). The dogs should have space to part from one another and come back at their own desire.

No matter the circumstance, you want your deaf dog to be safe and set him up for the greatest possibility of socializing success.

Group Training and the Dog Park

Many training facilities and big-box pet supply stores offer group training classes to help dogs learn basic commands and social skills. These classes can be an excellent way to introduce your deaf dog to other dogs in a controlled environment. The presence of an instructor can take the burden off you when it comes to reading your dog's cues and the cues of other canines.

Group training classes are limited in size, which can better guarantee a manageable number of other dogs (unlike the dog park).

I highly recommend bringing your dog to the dog park to help him build social skills, release pent-up energy, and have some fun. Despite the urge to jump in head-first, though, for the safety of your dog, go through the process of introducing him to the dog park slowly and with deliberate steps. Because dogs at the dog park are off-leash, if an incident occurs, it can be more difficult to control the situation.

Before your dog sets eyes on a potential dog park, scope it out alone. Go to the dog park several times during different times of the day. Park and go in. Take a moment to read the rules. Walk through the dog park to get an idea of how dogs react when you go through the gates. Note if they jump up on you and if their owners are nearby to control them. Chat with some of the dog owners to get a better idea of what the dog park is like. Don't be shy to ask them what they like and dislike about the park.

Most dog parks have peak hours. These often coincide with typical work hours and seasonal weather.

If you decide the dog park is a good fit for you and your deafie, schedule a time during non-peak hours to bring your dog.

Introduce your dog to the dog park by walking him on-leash around the outside. Let him approach other dogs that may run up to the fence. Notice if your dog hackles, growls, lunges, or barks. Bring your dog back several times to help acclimate him to being around other dogs through the safety of a fence. If your dog is consistently stiff or presents signs of aggression, fear, or discomfort, contact a trainer or behaviorist.

Dogs that demonstrate signs of excitement and friendliness are good candidates for the next steps. How do you know if your dog is happy, friendly, and excited? Tail wags and puppy-bows are excellent signs. A puppy bow is when your dog goes down on his front legs as a way to show other dogs he's not aggressive and wants to play. Some dogs will also whine as a way to show they desperately want to go inside and meet other dogs.

Bringing your dog back several times and keeping him outside of the dog park is a good idea. After this, you can bring your dog into the dog park, preferably when it is empty, so he can get the lay of the land. Even though he'll be by himself, your dog will likely enjoy taking in all the scents. (Note that you do not want to bring an unvaccinated or unaltered dog into a dog park).

The best time to introduce your dog to the dog park when there are other dogs present is during off-peak hours. This is often during the normal workday.

If you arrive during the workday and there is only one dog in the park, be sure to ask the owner if their dog is friendly. Sometimes other owners bring their nervous or possibly aggressive dogs during these times to enjoy some off-leash time.

When they've confirmed their dog is friendly, walk into the unleashing area and unleash your dog quickly. Spending too much time unleashing your dog can cause tension.

One mistake dog owners make is to bring their dog into a dog park with its leash on. They think it can help them control the situation better. In fact,

Photo Courtesy of Jane Hampson

FUN FACT
Plum

A deaf dog and her owner took the internet by the storm with an adorable viral video. The video depicts how Aiden Mann, a veterinary assistant, wakes his deaf Australian shepherd, Plum. In order not to startle her, Mann blows air on Plum gently to wake her. Mann employs a method of touch signals to communicate with Plum. The adorable pup now has an Instagram account (@ lola_plum365) which she shares with her dog sibling Lola, where the world can enjoy following their adventures.

many dogs in the dog park get even more excited and begin to surround a dog that is on-leash. This is also often true of dogs that get carried in or picked up by their owners. When a dog is on-leash, it can feel trapped or more vulnerable than if it were free to escape. If you are nervous about entering a dog park, take your time, and consider coming back when it's less busy. Do not bring your dog in on-leash.

Once your dog is unleashed, open the gate and watch his body language very carefully. Keep your dog's leash in your hand just in case. If your dog stiffens, hackles, growls, or shows his teeth, leash him up and walk away. If the dogs greeting your deafie show these signs, stay vigilant, and be ready to step in. Some normal cues and dog greetings include bottom-sniffing, tail-wagging, yipping, bowing, and relaxed body posture.

As your dog builds his social skills, you can begin to visit the dog park during busier times.

Common dog park etiquette includes not bringing treats into the park, treating others' dogs with the same courtesy you'd treat your own, picking up your dog's poo, and always keeping a close eye on your dog. Don't get distracted on your cell phone or leave your dog in the dog park and walk elsewhere.

Many people will tell you that children and dog parks are not the best combination. This is because children can be erratic and are eye-level with most dogs.

Read Your Dog's Body Language

A dog's social cues can be quite complex. Because dogs hunted in packs, they heavily relied on body language rather than verbal cues (although auditory cues are part of their communication). Learning these cues can give you greater insight into how your dog is feeling about a dog-to-dog interaction.

Tail-wagging:

Your dog is feeling emotion-ally excited. He's most likely happily excited, but not all the time.

Hackles:

Your dog has a line of fur that runs from the top of his neck to the base of his tail. This fur will stand up when your dog is aroused. It's similar to getting goose-bumps. If raised hackles are paired with teeth-baring, growling, or stiffness, your dog is upset. If your dog is simply hack-led, he may just be extremely excited.

Tucked tail (with possi-bly a tucked butt):

This indicates that your dog is fearful or nervous.

Cowering (possibly with lurching):

Your dog is scared and trying to make himself smaller to show that he's not a threat.

Rolling Over:

This is a sign of submission. Puppies and senior dogs tend to do this as a way to show they're not putting up any sort of fight.

Bowing:

Your dog wants to play.

Leaning forward:

This can be a sign of intimi-dation or excitement.

Sneezing during play:

This is a way dogs tell one another, "I'm just playing. This is simply play fighting, not the real thing."

Yawning:

Yawning can be a sign of stress or anxiety. Yawning floods the brain with oxygen, keeping your dog alert and on-edge.

Panting:

This can be a sign of nervousness and a way to increase oxygen to the brain. It is also a cooling mechanism for dogs.

Raising the Lip/ Showing the Teeth:

Your dog is warning others that he is unhappy with what's happening.

Maintained Eye Contact:

This can be a threatening and aggressive sign, especially if your dog shows the whites of his eyes.

Averting Eye Contact:

Your dog is calm and not confrontational.

Shaking:

This can be a way of releasing stress after the stressor has passed.

Pacing:

This is likely a sign of rest-lessness or anxiety.

Pet Siblings/Companion Pets

Many deaf dogs do extremely well when they have a canine sibling. A companion dog for your deafie can help him better interpret the world round him. As for other animal species, they can happily co-exist or even form a bond.

My deafie yields to his cat sister and gives her plenty of space. They do not snuggle or play together, though. A kitten raised with a deaf dog would possibly better adapt and form a stronger bond with a deafie.

Natchez heavily relies on his hearing brother, Fritz. If Fritz gets excited, Natchez gets excited. It Fritz barks at the mailman, Natchez is sure to join in, launching himself at the window to find out what's going on.

Fritz has a tendency to get annoyed with Natchez from time to time. It's important that your hearing dog get individual attention and some time and space apart from his deaf sibling.

Socializing a Dog with Acquired Deafness

Dogs with acquired deafness can be easy to startle. When socializing a dog with acquired deafness, it's best to find a play companion who is calm and around the same size. Some dogs with acquired deafness can react defensively out of fear.

I adopted a senior beagle with acquired deafness from old age and a lifetime of ear infections. She was extremely fearful when introduced to other dogs. She would lunge at their faces while yowling and snapping. Luckily, my other dogs were patient and seemed to understand that she posed no threat.

Like other deaf dogs, my beagle startles easily when touched and heavily relies on her senses of smell and sight.

When introducing a dog with acquired deafness to other dogs, it's always best to do so in a space where the deaf dog can retreat if necessary and see the other dog coming. Be prepared to step in if needed.

FUN FACT
Angelyne the Amazing Cattle Dog

Angelyne was born completely deaf, but that never stopped her and her owner/trainer Eric Melvin from giving over 500 inspiring public presentations as advocates for people and animals with disabilities. At her peak Angelyne had learned over 60 cues including hand signals, touch, scent, lights, body language, facial expressions and vibrations. Eric and Angelyne continued to perform and amaze crowds to spread her message until her death in 2020. Today Eric continues to carry on Angelyne's legacy as an advocate for Deaf dogs through his work with Maddie (Bottom Right) his new deaf ACD. You can read more about Eric, Angelyne, and Maddie at: www.ericandangelyne.com

CHAPTER 9
Living with a Deaf Dog

It will take some time for your deaf dog to settle into your home and get used to your routine. Most dogs take about three weeks to feel at home in their new environment.[1] Deaf dogs tend to surprise and seek a human to bond with, so don't be shocked if your deaf dog settles in more quickly. Of course, some deaf dogs may take a little longer, too.

This chapter is designed to help set you and your deaf dog up for success for the long-term, from often overlooked safety concerns to small gestures that show your deafie you care. Living with a deaf dog is both rewarding and offers long-lasting joy.

Safety

One of the most heartbreaking things I come across is deaf dogs picked up as strays and turned in to the local dog shelter. Many of these beautiful dogs faced a world full of dangers before being picked up, and, sadly, many will never leave the shelter after entering it. Which is to say, even if you have a fully fenced in yard and are a vigilant dog parent, I hope you will follow these safety tips in order to protect your precious pup.

A Leash Is Always a Safe Measure

When you take your deaf dog on walks, it's a no-brainer to leash him up, right? While most that read this book will agree that leashes are one of the best tools to protect their dogs, circumstances will arise where you may feel tempted to let your deafie off-leash. Try your hardest to resist the urge to let your deafie run free. It could save your dog's life and save you countless moments of stress and headaches. Some scenarios include hiking, going to the beach, and going to the lake.

When I think about the problem of letting a deafie off-leash, one scenario comes to mind. One summer, I went to the dog park with Natchez and his brother, Fritz. The park was empty, so we decided to hike on the adjacent, fully fenced-in trail. I let Natchez and Fritz off-leash and began walking.

---

1   "For All Creatures Great and Small," Royal Society for the Prevention of Cruelty to Animals, accessed December 21, 2020, https://www.rspca.org.au/sites/default/files/website/Adopt-a-pet/Your-new-dog/FOR%20ACT%20Your%20new%20dog%20tips.pdf.

Natchez stayed in-sight for the majority of the hike, but it was hot, and he started to slow down toward the end. I let him trail behind. By the time I got back to the entrance, Natchez was nowhere to be found. I began circling back, looking for him. Well, I had to completely re-walk the trail in reverse because he got frightened at some point and ran reverse of the trail. While this wasn't the most dangerous of situations, it was very, very hot out, which could have resulted in heatstroke. I did feel helpless, scared, and frustrated at myself, though.

HELPFUL TIP
Dog Strollers

Deaf dogs can be easily startled when suddenly approached by a stranger or dog. If your deaf dog is a small breed, he might feel more comfortable in a doggy stroller while running errands in crowded areas. The canopy and enclosed area in a dog stroller provides a space with lower stimulation and a greater sense of safety for your dog. Getting your dog acclimated to a new stroller can be a bit of a process, but positive reinforcement and repetition are the key to any new routine.

Going to Dog Parks

The exception to the rule is the dog park. If you are comfortable and confident with your deaf dog's social skills, then allow your deafie to enjoy some freedom at the dog park. In my experience, leashes can be a trigger to the other dogs that there's a newbie among them. Leashes can also make the leashed dog feel trapped since they cannot escape and react out of fear. If you do let your deaf dog frolic among other dogs at the dog park, do not leave your leash at the front. Keep it with you at all times, and always keep a mindful eye on your dog and the others.

Dog Park Dangers

Because deafies can be socially awkward, other dogs may pick up on these differences, target your deafie, and exhibit bullying-type behaviors. This often includes getting mounted (or humped). While this isn't the most pleasant sight, it is relatively normal. There are two issues with ignoring the behavior, though. First, your deafie may get offended and react negatively to being mounted, and secondly, humping dogs can dig into the sides, hips, or belly of their victim with their dew claws or claws, leaving scratches and bruises.

Should you remove the humping perpetrator from your dog? Use your judgment when it comes to other dogs at the park. In the best-case scenario, the offending dog's owner is nearby and will pull the dog off and away from

yours. If you must physically remove the other dog from yours, be gentle, use their collar, and be respectful. People tend to get a bit sensitive about how their dog is handled.

You can also simply remove your dog from the situation and relocate to another side of the park. If the mounting continues or your park isn't big enough to get away from the situation, leave and take your dog on a walk nearby, instead.

While dog parks can offer an amazing opportunity for your dog to practice socializing in a controlled environment, it's vital to keep in mind that there can be misunderstandings between dogs and tussles or even fights.

To give you an idea of what can go wrong at the dog park, I will use Natchez's experience as an example. He has gotten into two misunderstandings at the dog park.

The first occurred when an owner arrived with two Huskies. It was quite obvious the owner was nervous. He kept both of his dogs on-leash in the little pen between the entrance and the main part of the park. The dogs already in the park, including Natchez, were quite excited to greet the newcomers. They all gathered around the pen, barking and excitedly waiting for them to enter. This, naturally, made the owner even more nervous, elongating the time he spent in the pen. This multiplied the anxiety of his dogs. By the time he unleashed them and opened the gate, his male dog rushed at Natchez, snarling and biting his ears. Natchez, terrified by the whole thing, was able to get away pretty quickly. I left, surveyed Natchez for damage—his ear was cut, but he was otherwise fine, and I left for the day.

Another incident occurred at another dog park months later. Natchez was happily sniffing around at the back of the park when a Doberman with casted ears startled him. Natchez gruffed and then tried to initiate play. The Doberman did not like this idea (likely because his ears were in pain) and cowered. The owner ran over to retrieve his dog, saying some nasty things about Natchez as he did so. Obviously, he should have never brought his dog in ear casts to the park, but that is the type of thing that does happen since dog parks are often unsupervised by any official or authority.

What Should You Do if a Fight Does Occur?

If a scuffle ever breaks out, do not stick your hand between the dogs. This could result in a serious injury. The best ways to break up a dog fight include throwing water or a blanket on the dogs. If your dog park has a hose, this is likely the best way to intervene. If the dogs separate, be ready to step in, leash up your dog, and leave. Once you're in a safe place, survey your dog for injury.

Note that if a dog has latched onto another, yanking the dog can tear the victim's skin. If this happens, try to get the dog to loosen his jaw and let go. Be ready to immediately pull the other dog away.

Other Notes on the Dog Park

Be aware that dog parks sometimes foster bad habits. Because the dog park fosters pack mentality, dogs can 'gang up' or learn behaviors you may find unsavory. Some dogs learn to hump others at the dog park. Other bad habits include getting overly excited when a dog is picked up or brought into the park on-leash.

Furthermore, many dog parks have rules against unfixed female dogs but disregard that unfixed male dogs can exhibit aggressive tendencies.

Additionally, I've seen countless dogs with fleas at the dog park. Do not let your dog go without flea prevention if you're planning a trip to the dog park.

Dog parks are not right for every dog. Your dog can still learn social skills by going to doggie daycare, training, or small playdates.

Photo Courtesy
of Mary Thompson

Deaf Dog Harnesses and Equipment

You can find a wide array of deaf dog gear for sale online. This includes identifying leashes, harnesses, collars, and more. I have yet to find a deaf dog harness that is more than just embroidered fabric. I still put Natchez in his deaf dog harness/vest when going into a situation where identifying him as deaf is helpful. I do not attach his leash to the harness, though. It's just a signifier.

The biggest benefit of a vest that identifies your dog as deaf is that people are less likely to run up and pet your deafie without your permission. I have noticed it doesn't prevent kids from approaching, though.

Watch for Cars, Kids, Other Dogs on Walks

When you take your deaf dog on walks, keep in mind that you're responsible for your dog's safety. This means that you must remain aware of your surroundings, watch for dangers, and know how to react should any arise.

When it comes to cars, your deaf dog cannot hear them coming. This means you must be mindful to not let your deafie walk into the road before you're ready to cross, and you must keep him or her a safe distance from traffic. One practice you can get into is having your deafie sit and wait at intersections. The "sit" and "stay" commands followed by a release sign are the easiest way to do this.

One of the most common things you will run into is kids sprinting toward you and your deaf dog. While most kids are harmless and many deaf dogs adore little ones, you do not want children (especially those unaccompanied by an adult) petting your dog on walks. Kids tend to come on strong and fast. They also have a tendency to lunge straight for a dog's head or be a bit rough. This can make your deafie nervous, and the last thing you want is your deaf dog becoming needlessly fearful of kids or nipping a child.

To prevent kids from petting your dog without permission, be sure to call to them before they approach too closely. I simply say, "Hey, my dog is nervous and doesn't want to be pet right now." This works. I usually add, "maybe another time" to soften the blow.

If you know the approaching child, their parent is present, and you are 100% confident your dog will be okay getting pet remind the child that your dog cannot hear. Try to avoid saying, "My dog is deaf," since most kids don't exactly know what that means. Instead, say, "my dog cannot hear, so please go slow. Let him/her smell your hand and avoid petting his/her head." I usually plan for petting sessions by bringing treats. I let the kids put their hands flat with a treat on it and tell them to let Natchez approach them.

When it comes to kids, you are always better safe than sorry. Do not hesitate to tell a child they may not pet your dog. It is also okay to turn around on a walk to avoid kids if you do not want them running up to your dog. Your dog's safety and the safety of children should always be a top priority.

One of the most stressful things that happens on our walks is when another dog is off leash. Never trust a dog you don't know. Should you see a dog unleashed, turn around and walk away. If the dog runs at you or approaches, call for its owner. I have had this happen with two off-leash Dobermans. They were huge and squaring off with my dogs. I yelled, "Please come get your dogs!" and "Your dogs are threatening my dogs." The owner called her dogs home.

If you live in a rural area where people often let their dogs wander, you may want to carry a spray bottle of water with you.

Finally, always know your city or county's leash laws. If you see a dog wandering around lost or posing a threat to people or pets, call the authorities.

Communicating with Your Neighbors

When adopting a deafie, it's important to let your neighbors know about the new addition to your household. This will give them a heads up that they may hear barking, and if your deafie were to ever escape your yard, they'd know where to return your dog should they find him or her.

Photo Courtesy of Cindy Nelson

"I'm Deaf" Notice on ID Tag and Microchip

You should order an ID tag and have your deaf dog microchipped as soon as you can after adoption. A microchip and ID tag can help you reunite with your deaf dog much more quickly should he or she go missing. Remember to update your dog's microchip information if you move or your phone number changes.

I often read about dogs being brought into vets, having their chips scanned, and the chip not being registered. This is a travesty. Many adopted dogs come microchipped, but you may have to update the information in the microchip database. Do not put off or skip this important step in keeping your dog safe.

On your dog's ID tag, include the words, "I am deaf" in addition to your dog's name, your phone number, and even your address. Natchez's ID tag reads, "I'm deaf, patience plz."

I recommend a tag rather than an embroidered ID collar because people are more likely to approach and corral a dog if they can see that he or she has an ID tag. Embroidered collars are a great back up, though, should your dog go missing and break off his or her ID tag.

Getting a Deaf Dog's Attention

One of the biggest handicaps of not hearing is your deafie doesn't know when you call his or her name. This can become a hazard should your dog sneak out of the house and run toward the road. Vibration training can be an unbeatable tool should this happen. Of course, you would need to have the remote for the collar on you at the time. If your dog does run towards a road or another danger, you will have to catch up to him or her, get between your dog and the danger, and signal for them to stop by putting your hand up.

Should you want to get your deafie's attention when he or she is far away, waving your hands is usually pretty effective. You can then signal to your dog to "come" by waving them toward you (similar to how you would tell a vehicle to 'back-up') or by lowering yourself with open arms. You can also use your porch light if you have a large backyard to get your dog's attention when it's time to come inside at night.

To get your dog's attention while he or she is relaxing in the house, you can wave or gently tap your dog's shoulder. Putting a flat hand on your dog's should or back is another option. Always be gentle.

CHAPTER 10
Promoting Comfort and Emotional Security for Your Deafie

All dogs have their quirks when it comes to being comfortable. Some prefer lying on tile rather than a fluffy bed, while others love to be tucked in under a blanket. With time you will learn what works best for your deaf dog. Here are some tips that work for most in situations that may make some dogs uneasy.

How to Meet and Greet a Deaf Dog

Most dogs prefer to come to you for introductions. The same is often true for deafies. When people meet your deafie, ask them to go slow or wait for the dog to approach them. They should not make rapid or exaggerated hand movements since this can be scary or could confuse a dog whose primary means of communication with people is hand signals. (You'll learn that your friends that talk with their hands may be quite confusing to your deafie). The deafie may sniff the new person then back away, or they may pause for pets. Advise the new person to avoid petting your dog's head since this can be frightening to a dog.

If your dog backs away, that's okay. Let him. Just go about your business, ignoring your deafie, but allowing him to approach the stranger in their own time at their own comfort level.

HELPFUL TIP
Night-Light

Since deaf dogs rely more heavily on sight than hearing dogs, providing a gentle night-light in your dog's sleeping area may help your dog feel safe. If your dog is in the habit of checking up on you during the night, a night-light might provide an extra level of comfort to a dog who can't rely on hearing to do so.

Sitting down within eye-sight of your deafie tells your dog that they're comfortable, sticking around for a bit, and mean no harm. Avoiding eye contact with a nervous dog can also make a stranger more approachable. Holding a treat in a flat palm is always encouraging for skittish dogs as well.

Never force your dog to greet someone new or be petted by a stranger if your dog is too nervous.

How to Wake a Deaf Dog

Deaf dogs often sleep very deeply. Without being able to hear, they will sleep through the opening of your door, through you calling their name, and even through a fire alarm. Because they conch out you want to be gentle when waking them, since deafies tend to startle when awoken.

When your deafie is asleep, turning a light on may wake them. Otherwise, you will gently want to tap or rest a hand on your dog's shoulder. I often stroke Natchez from the top of his shoulders down. With time, your dog will learn this form of touch is you and be less startled when waking.

Photo Courtesy
of Jean Jacobs

Photo Courtesy of Jane Hampson

Deaf Dogs and Routine

All dogs thrive on routine. When your dog has a set schedule, they feel more secure. They know what to expect and when. This stability is the best thing a deaf dog owner can provide.

Begin establishing your dog's routine as soon as you can. Stick to a convenient mealtime, walk time, and even bathroom breaks at regular intervals. If your schedule does not allow for a perfectly conforming schedule, then do your best to keep mealtimes and walks as consistent as possible.

When a major change occurs in your dog's life, keeping as much of his or her schedule normal can help him adjust more quickly. This includes having houseguests, using a dog sitter, and moving. The less that changes, the more confident and secure your dog will feel. Think of it as them thinking to themselves, "Well, there's a new person in the house, but at least I know when I'll be fed and walked."

You can make certain accommodations to help keep your dog's schedule during times that require change, such as the holidays or when starting a new job. Hiring a dog walker can help keep your dog's schedule more consist. Setting up an automatic dog feeder can also help keep meals consistent if you won't be home to feed your dog at his regular mealtime.

Comfort Sweaters and Vests

What is your natural instinct when it comes to calming a nervous dog? Often talking in a calming voice is the first thing people try. For obvious reasons, this may not be the best option for your deaf dog. Comfort vests like the Thunder Vest or just a sweater can help a deaf dog feel more relaxed.

Natchez loves wearing sweaters, although the Thunder Vest never did much for him. His trainer explained to me that the sweater acts as a reassuring and calming 'hug-like' sensation for him. They also come in handy when it's cold out or in snow. A sweater can be a great go-to during travel or other semi-stressful situations if your deaf dog has an affinity for them.

HELPFUL TIP
Overcoming Separation Anxiety

Deaf dogs may be more prone to developing separation anxiety. Early crate training is a great way to counter the development of this behavior. If your deaf dog is exhibiting signs of separation anxiety, you can practice leaving your dog alone in a safe environment, such as his crate, for short periods of time, then increase the length of time as your dog becomes more comfortable. Providing your dog with a shirt you've worn and that smells like you is another great way to provide comfort for your anxious dog during times apart.

CHAPTER 11
Understanding the Personality Traits of a Deaf Dog

N o two deaf dogs are the same, but you can bet your deafie will have a unique personality. Deafies are often described as "quirky" and "goofy." Some are more aloof, while others are spunky and peppy. While you will get a preview of your dog's personality when you meet him or her and bring them home, only time will fully reveal the depth of your dog's full personality.

There are a few common personality traits you can count on, though.

Deaf Dogs are Observant and Pick Up on Patterns

I continue to be caught off guard by how observant Natchez is and how astute he is when it comes to predicting my actions. He can tell the difference between when I'm leaving the house to run an errand versus just going out to water the plants. When I'm leaving for errands, he will put himself to bed before I even walk out of the door, but if I'm stepping out to check mail or water plants, he will wait at the top of the stairs.

By picking up on minute differences in my actions, he knows what to expect. Your deafie will likely be similar.

Anticipate your dog learning where treats are stored, when you're getting ready for a walk or ready for bed, and other common daily routines. And don't be surprised when your deafie knows what you're going to do before you do it. They have a knack for this.

HELPFUL TIP
Deaf Dogs and Unwanted Barking

Whether your dog is hearing or not, you may struggle with controlling his barking. There are many methods for using positive reinforcement to train deaf dogs not to bark, but before starting on any of these, you should consider what could be causing this behavior. Frustration, anxiety, pain, and discomfort are all potential causes for barking. If you've ruled out all of these, your dog's barking may be a learned behavior. Interacting with your deaf dog while he is barking may only encourage him to do it more frequently, so be sure to wait for your dog to be quiet before engaging with him.

Photo Courtesy of Lara DePietro

Don't Expect a Greeting at the Door

One of the eeriest aspects of owning a deafie is that some of the normal 'dog behaviors' just don't happen. If your deaf dog is a single pet, don't expect him or her to greet you at the door. In fact, for the first few weeks and months, you may have to seek out your deafie to find where he or she has fallen asleep. This can be a little frightening to some new owners since it can feel like your dog may have snuck out or escaped.

Even some deafies with siblings will sleep through their owners arriving home. It all depends if they sleep close enough for the other dogs' action to wake them.

This can come in handy when you are expecting guests. You can let your deaf dog sleep through their arrival if you choose, so your guest can easily enter the house without being sniffed and licked by an excited dog.

Deaf Dogs Are Deep Sleepers

I often have to go and wake Natchez up to let him know it's time to go out to use the potty or to let him know something important is going on. Almost all deafies sleep very, very deeply.

Some deafies prefer to block off other senses to receive deeper, more restful sleep. This may be because their other senses become more attuned to subtle changes, so they are more easily alerted to slight changes in pressure, temperature, and light. When Natchez goes to sleep for the night, he prefers to be fully covered by a blanket to help block out light. I imagine it's like a sensory deprivation chamber in some ways.

You will also notice when your deafie wakes, he or she will likely scan his or her surroundings to see what is going on. When you first bring your deafie home, he may also want to physically walk or run through the house when he wakes to check on things.

"Doing Rounds" Around the House

Normal dogs often rely on their sense of hearing to know what's going on out of their line of vision. Deafies do not have this ability. Instead, they have to rely on their sense of smell and vision. This leads to a common but peculiar habit of running through the house and checking rooms. Once a deafie becomes more acquainted with his home, this habit will likely fall away, but it will re-emerge if you move, bring your deafie on vacation, or if you have a guest or visitor.

While strange, running between rooms does make sense if you think about it from the perspective of a deaf dog. How do they know your guest isn't just in another room?

Natchez has the habit of running down the hall, sticking his head in the doorway of each room to figure out where I am.

Deafies Mimic Their Hearing Peers

Many deaf dogs pick up on the actions of their hearing counterparts and instinctually parrot their actions. This can include lunging at a squirrel that one of the other dogs sees, barking at the mailman, or barking from behind a fence as a stranger passes.

You will notice your deafie watching his dog siblings and friends for clues as to what's happening.

Excuse You! Deafies Can Come Across as Rude

Because deaf dogs tend to be clingy, their need and desire to be in one's personal space can come across as rude. Don't be surprised if your deafie climbs onto the back of the sofa behind you or a guest, climbs onto the arm of the sofa, lies on your guests' feet, or tries to get onto a chair that is too small for a human plus a deaf dog.

You may need to remind guests to close doors tightly if your deafie develops the habit of looking in rooms or pushing doors open. There is a very good chance your deafie will follow a guest to the restroom and proceed to try to follow them in or push the door open.

Deaf dogs can also be considered silly or rude when it comes to loudly passing gas and burping. They can't help it, though. I still crack up whenever Natchez lets one loudly rip while staring off into space as if nothing happened.

Many deafies also come across as nosey because they like watching out of the window. They will peep around curtains or push aside blinds to be a self-appointed neighborhood watch.

Eric and Angelyne

Trancing

FUN FACT

Aggression Myth

There's a long-standing myth that deaf dogs are more aggressive than their hearing counterparts. As many deaf dog owners can attest, this simply isn't true. The myth likely originated because of a deaf dog's tendency toward "startle aggression," meaning that it's easier to startle a deaf dog than its hearing counterparts, and any startled dog may react with aggression. With proper training and care, deaf dogs are just as kind and loving as any other dog.

Do you know that feeling when you have your back scratched? It's quite nice, right? Well, many dogs (and deaf dogs) really like that feeling as well. Some like it so much so that it puts them into a meditative state that is often referred to as "trancing" or "ghost walking." When I first found Natchez trancing, I worried he was having a seizure since they can look similar, but I quickly learned he was not. I called this behavior "lizarding" because his walking looked very similar to how a chameleon walks. He continues to trance in the backyard, on hikes, and in my in-laws' home beneath their house plants.

When Natchez first started trancing, I Googled it, and at the time, there was no information on this odd behavior. Luckily, now, more dog parents have reported and recorded their dogs trancing, and there is more information on trancing, including a study done on Bull Terriers by Bull Terrier Neurological Disorder Resources (BTNDR). BTNDR[1] concluded that trancing is not a neurological disorder or side effect of a brain abnormality. It is a harmless tactile sensation that relaxes the dog and feels good.

Trancing isn't just joy from their owners scratching their backs, though. It often only requires the slightest tickle from branches, curtains, low-hanging clothes on a line, bushes, or even a tablecloth. A dog that trances will look as if they're walking in slow motion. They may even bounce, rock, or sway a bit while doing so.

If your dog does this, do not panic. He is okay. I do have trouble getting Natchez's attention while he's "in the zone." So, I often have to retrieve him and gently pet him to help him find his way back to reality. It's okay to snap your dog out of trancing by gently caressing his shoulder.

---

1   "BTNDR Poll: Trancing in Bull Terriers," Bull Terrier Neurological Disorder Resources, accessed December 20, 2020http://web.archive.org/web/20140428063553/http://www.btneuro.org/btneuro-old/trancing_poll.htm.

Deafies Are Affectionate and Devoted to Their Owners

As I've pointed out several times throughout this book, it's hard to find a more snuggly, attached, devoted dog than a deafie. Don't be surprised when your deaf dog follows you into the bathroom and lies right outside the bathtub or shower as you bathe. They tend to like to be in the same room as their owners. He or she will likely invite themselves into your bed at night and into the front seat on road trips.

A lot of deaf dogs like to maintain physical contact with their people, as well. They will lean into your legs, side, or even try to climb on your lap when given the chance.

If you want your deafie to be more independent, you will want to work on these habits from the time you bring him or her home.

CHAPTER 12
Providing for Your Deaf Dog's Health

Meeting your deaf dog's daily needs is the first step to a happy, healthy dog, but you will also want to account for their long-term health needs, as well. The more proactive you are, the better your dog's health will likely be. This chapter will cover those proactive measures that can extend your dog's life and keep him mentally stimulated for years to come. Of course, in addition to providing your dog the best quality of life, preventative health provisions can reduce future vet bills and make dog ownership the best experience it can be.

Exercise

An active dog is a healthy dog. Regular exercise through walks and play help your deaf dog maintain healthy muscles, joints, skeletal health, mental health, and coordination. Most dogs need between an hour to two hours of active play and exercise daily. You will want to consult your dog's specific breed guide or ask your vet if you're unsure of how much exercise your dog should get each day.

Cardio can help keep your dog in shape and prevent your dog from becoming overweight to obese. Preventing obesity can lengthen your dog's lifespan and improve their wellbeing. If your deafie tends to be more aloof, you will want to encourage longer walks to make up for their lack of play. Walks help burn calories, elevate the heart rate, and provide your dog with mental stimulation. All deaf dogs should go on daily walks to prevent boredom and depression. Going in the backyard for bathroom breaks is not enough exercise for most dogs, even in the winter.

Remember to check your deafie's paw pads periodically through the week to ensure they're in good health. If you notice any cracks, scrapes, or cuts, discontinue walks until they heal. Avoid walking on ice melts and rock salt in the winter, as well, to protect your pup's pads. If you live in an extreme climate, paw balm can protect your dog's paws from cracking and minor burns.

If you are physically unable to provide your dog with long walks, consider hiring a dog walker and engaging your dog in other forms of play. Some other exercise alternatives can include playing with toys indoors, playdates with other dogs, and treat hide-and-seek. Deafies are usually suckers for treat hide-and-seek since they're so food motivated, and their senses of smell

*Photo Courtesy
of Morgan Elizabeth*

HELPFUL TIP
Leashing Tips

Exercise is an important part of any dog's life, whether he's deaf or not. A general rule of thumb for deaf dogs is that they shouldn't be let off-leash in unenclosed areas, such as parks or open fields. Once your dog is an adult and is well-trained to check in with you at frequent intervals, you might be able to reconsider this rule, depending on the laws and rules in your area. Many deaf dog owners choose an extra-long or extendable leash for outdoor activities. This gives their dog room to play but allows the owner to still safely maintain control of the dog and keep him out of danger.

are so poignant. To play this simple game, put your deafie in another room. Then hide training treats under furniture, in blankets, wherever you think would make good hiding spots. Then let your deafie in the room and watch him sniff out some fun and tasty treats.

Puppies, while more active, should not partake in high-impact exercise that could hurt their developing joints and bones. This means deafies under six to nine months old should not be long-distance running buddies. If you want to start a running routine with your dog, ask your vet if he or she is ready and healthy enough.

Some brachycephalic breeds (breeds with short snouts) should never go running, especially when it's hot out. They can easily overheat and may even suffocate from not getting enough air.

It's vital that senior dogs stay active, as well. Regular activity and strengthening the muscles while keeping joints loose and lubricated can prevent slips, trips, sprains, and stave off dementia.

Diet

Feeding your dog a healthy, well-balanced diet is important. Sometimes it can be difficult to distinguish what food would be best for your deafie, though, just based on the front of the package. When choosing a food, be sure to read over the ingredient list. Select a food with real meat as the first ingredient listed and try to avoid a food with a laundry list of preservatives or fillers. Beware of foods that list soy, corn, or wheat too high on the ingredient list. These are fillers that will help your dog feel full temporarily but do not do much nutritionally. Additionally, some brands will sell a "high-protein" food that is supplemented with pea-derived protein. This can be a red flag that they are trying to charge more for a higher protein food, but pea protein does not contain amino acids, nor does it have the same biological value as real meat.

Additionally, you want to avoid dog foods that overly rely on byproducts. Byproducts are usually non-muscle-based meat like organs, cartilage, some bone, etc. Your deafie would have eaten these had he hunted down prey in the wild, so they're not harmful. But you do want to be sure your dog receives higher-quality meat in his primary food, as well.

If you're not sure, always choose a food that is AAFCO balanced. The AAFCO, or Association of American Feed Control Officials, has an established set of standards or profiles that describe what an animal feed needs in order for its intended consumer species to thrive. This is to say, that when a food is labeled as meeting the AAFCO standards, it meets all of your dog's basic nutritional needs.

Be cautious when it comes to trends and specialty dog diets. All-meat diets or completely grain-free diets can pose health risks. Dogs need veggies, fruits, vitamins, and minerals to survive.

You can also select a food for your dog's specific age, breed, and dietary needs.

Puppies need a special diet until they're about six-to-nine months old. Older dogs often need foods that are easier to chew and digest. Luckily, most foods tailor their recipes and label their foods for your dog's specific dietary specs. You will want to use a puppy food that reflects the size of your dog since the nutrients are formulated to help your dog grow at the appropriate rate.

If you are unsure of your dog's dietary needs, or you suspect your dog has a food allergy, consult your vet for help.

Photo Courtesy of Lisa Chiado

Mental Wellbeing

When it comes to your dog's overall health, mental wellbeing plays a major role in how he feels day-to-day and in the long run. You want to keep your deafie mentally and physically active. The old saying that a busy dog is a good dog is accurate. When dogs get bored, they tend to get into more mischief. And in the long run, a dog that is bored day in and day out can become more anxious and depressed. Studies also show that dogs that receive mental stimulation stay more mentally sharp and can slow the progression of dementia.[1]

One of the best ways to keep your dog mentally stimulated is through daily training. This can be working on behaviors your dog already knows, building on those tricks, or learning new tricks and combinations of tricks.

Walks expose your dog to new scenery, scents, and more. This engages their minds and imaginations. Regular training and games can help provide your dog with a healthy outlet for their mental energy as well. Even allowing your dog access to watch out the window can provide additional mental stimulation for a bored deafie. Most importantly, remember to introduce new toys, games, and experiences into your deafie's life.

HELPFUL TIP
Special Medical Concerns

Deafness in dogs does not usually correlate with an increased risk for any other health concerns. However, since deaf dogs are often white, these dogs may require extra care in the sun because white dogs are more prone to sunburn. If you have a white deafie, consider using a dog-safe sunscreen or investing in protective clothing such as a UV-blocking suit or a sun shirt made for dogs.

Hands-down, Natchez loves walks more than anything else in the world. He lights up when he sees the leash come out. Natchez also adores treat puzzles and practicing his signs.

Dogs can also suffer from depression and anxiety that won't go away on their own. If this is the case for your dog, make an appointment with your vet. There is a wide range of prescriptions that can support your dog's emotional and mental health.

1   Jodi Helmer, "Brain Games: Mental Stimulation Keeps Dogs Minds Sharp," WebMD, March 6, 2019, https://pets.webmd.com/dogs/features/mental-stimulation-sharpens-dogs-minds

Medicine and Vet Visits

Find a good vet. I've learned that the right vet can make a world of difference when caring for a deaf dog. While deaf dogs don't necessarily require additional veterinary care, a good vet can support you throughout your dog's life. Always ask about their experience with deaf dogs and see how you jive with your vet. When you go in for your dog's appointment, pay attention to how clean, organized, and well-staffed a practice is. If you don't feel comfortable with a vet, don't feel like you're not allowed to switch practices.

Remember to check with friends and family for veterinary recommendations.

Signs of a good veterinary practice include:

- a clean facility
- enough staff to keep up with clients (the reception area shouldn't resemble a sardine can filled to the brim with pets and their owners)
- clear communication
- not feeling rushed during your dog's exam
- being able to ask questions
- explaining your options thoroughly

During veterinary visits, always ask any questions you may have about your dog's health and behavior. Most vets are a wealth of knowledge when it comes to understanding your dog's actions. It's even okay to simple ask "Is _____ normal?"

Most dogs require annual exams. Puppies and elderly dogs may need more visits. Once a dog is over eight or nine, you may want to increase regular checkups to twice annually.

Your vet will inform you as to what vaccines and preventative medications are best for your dog. Some deaf dog activists argue that many prescriptions and treatments are not safe for deaf dogs since they're not tested on deaf dogs. That being said, I would never let one of my dogs go without heartworm, tick, and flea prevention.

CHAPTER 13

Letting Your Dog Cross the Rainbow Bridge

A s your deaf dog ages, a time may arise that you wonder if your dog's quality of life has declined to the point where euthanasia may be an option. Sometimes, owners are not sure how to tell if their dog is still enjoying life or if an expensive medical procedure is the right choice. This chapter should give you some clarity on when it's time to say "Goodbye!" to your best friend.

Assessing Your Deafie's Quality of Life

One of the biggest travesties is that our dogs cannot speak to us. They cannot tell us they're in pain or that they just feel miserable. This can make it difficult to tell whether or not a dog is suffering.

There is no perfect answer for whether it's time to consider letting your dog cross the Rainbow Bridge, but there are some factors you can look at to decide how much your dog is still enjoying his life.

- If your dog cannot move around freely or independently, it's a sign that he's unable to fully partake in life and activities that most dogs enjoy. Dogs that can go on walks, play, and swim at about half the level or length that they used to are still mobile and independent enough to enjoy life.

- Dogs with chronic or acute pain that cannot be controlled by medication may be suffering. If your dog refuses to move or cries or whines from pain, it may be time to talk to the vet.

FUN FACT
Deaf Dog Longevity

The life expectancy of a deaf dog is usually no different than that of a hearing one. A dog's life expectancy can be estimated based on its breed and health history. In general, smaller breeds tend to live longer than larger breeds, and this is also true for deaf dogs. Some people believe that deaf dogs are more likely to be hit by a car because they can't hear it approaching, but this is a myth. A busy road is dangerous for any off-leash dog, and no dog is born knowing that the street is potentially dangerous. The longest-lived dog, according to the Guinness World Records, was an Australian cattle dog named Bluey who lived to be 29 years old.

- Pay attention to your dog's ability to breathe and eat. Difficulty breathing or refusal to eat or drink are bad signs that call for immediate medical attention. If your dog's condition cannot be treated, it may be best to consider letting him pass on comfortably.

- One sign of diminished quality of life that many dog parents do know about is a dog's inability to control elimination. Urinating or defecating uncontrollably for an extended period is a clear sign that a dog's health has gone downhill.

Your dog may also contract a fatal disease, a progressive or hard to treat disease, or be involved in a traumatic and severe accident. If this happens, be sure to discuss your pet's prognosis, future veterinary needs, extent of recovery, and cost with your vet. Have a discussion with your family members regarding your budget and the care needed for your dog. If you believe it is within your means and ability, and your dog will likely live a happy, healthy life, go for it. If you are uncertain, try consulting your vet again with any additional questions you may have that will shine light on the situation. If you cannot afford your pet's medical treatment, yet the vet says your dog has a high chance of recovery and potential quality of life, you can consider using a payment plan. Or if you cannot afford care, but your dog's quality of life would be good after treatment, you can contact local shelters to ask if they would take your in dog as a surrender, provided the veterinary care,

then adopt your dog out. Another option for providing your pet with a medical procedure you cannot afford is to contact your local Humane Society, Animal Care and Control, or a veterinary non-profit to see if they can offer the veterinary procedure at reduced cost.

How to Say "Goodbye"

Know that the decision to say "Goodbye" is never easy. The process of letting go and celebrating your dog's life can help.

If you decide euthanasia is the most humane option for your dog, decide how to spend your dog's final days. Consider creating a memorial or doing a project to preserve the best memories you've shared with your furry best friend. You can create a paw print impression, take photos with your dog, or plant a memorial tree or shrub together. You can also visit your dog's favorite places to go and let him partake in some special treats and activities.

Kids also need time to say their goodbyes with your dog. It can be difficult to explain to children that it's your dog's time to pass on. There are many excellent book options designed to teach and comfort children of all ages. Some that I recommend include:

- *Saying Goodbye to Lulu* **by Corinne Demas**
- *Dog Heaven* **by Cynthia Rylant**

- *My Pet Memory Book* **by S. Wallace**
- *The Rainbow Bridge: A Visit to Pet Paradise* **by Adrian Raeside**
- *The Invisible Leash* **by Patrice Karst and Joanne Lew-Vrienthoff**

One thing you will also want to decide is whether you want to be present in the veterinary room during your dog's passing. While this may seem traumatic, many owners gain a lot of closure by being able to dote on, pet, and comfort their dog. Being present also comforts many dog parents because they know their dog wasn't in pain during the process or alone during their last breaths. When making up your mind, know that euthanasia is a painless process, and you will not witness your dog suffering.

After Your Dog Has Passed

Prepare for the grieving process after your dog's passing. You will grieve. The grieving process is different for everyone. Expect to feel sad, angry, and confused. Know that it is okay to talk about your dog and continue to share stories of the happy memories you had with him. Holding an intimate memorial service with friends and family can help you process the loss, as well.

Don't hesitate to contact a therapist should you become depressed or overwhelmed with emotion. Taking a few days off work can also help you meditate on your dog's life and role in your life.

Resist adopting another dog while you are still grieving. This can be disastrous for you and the adoptee. No dog will ever replace yours, and you need time to heal.

Dogs fill our lives with joy and light, and when they're gone, their absence is deeply felt.

Life as a Deaf Dog Owner

I hope you enjoy life with your deaf dog. There's no doubt that deaf dogs make great pets for many people and families. They're loving and quirky and will light up your days with laughter. As a proud deaf dog owner, I can say that having Natchez in my life has been one of the most rewarding experiences I have had.

Made in the USA
Monee, IL
02 July 2021

c5c18e0f-bbd5-4ce8-9849-d0d58f88b316R01